# CONNECT

## MASTERING THE ART OF EFFECTIVE COMMUNICATION

PROF SOUJANYA PUDI

INDIA • SINGAPORE • MALAYSIA

ISBN 979-8-89066-871-4

# Dedication

To my Guru Sri Sathya Sai Baba

My parents who allowed me to express my views freely ....power of communication

My family Anil, Sindz & Sidz thank you for your endless encouragement and belief in my abilities.

Your love and understanding have been my pillars of strength throughout this creative endeavour.

To my mentors and team at NSHM your guidance and wisdom have shaped me into the writer I am today. Your invaluable lessons and constructive criticism have pushed me to constantly strive for excellence.

And finally, to the beauty of Communication itself - a timeless gift that transcends boundaries and connects us all.

May this dedication be a tribute to the magic of words, the joy of reading, and the profound impact that books can have on our lives.

With deepest gratitude,

**Prof Soujanya Pudi**

# Contents

# Foreword

In a world that is increasingly connected, effective communication has become paramount. Our ability to express ourselves clearly, listen actively, and understand one another is critical for navigating the complexities of modern life. Whether in personal relationships, professional settings, or even in the digital realm, the power of communication cannot be overstated.

This book serves as a guide on the journey towards becoming a skilled communicator. It delves into the art of conveying ideas, emotions, and information with clarity and impact. By exploring various aspects of communication, it equips readers with the tools and techniques necessary to forge strong connections, resolve conflicts, and build meaningful relationships.

From the art of persuasion to active listening, from non-verbal cues to virtual communication, this book covers a wide range of topics that are essential for effective communication in today's diverse and ever-evolving world. It offers practical tips, insightful anecdotes, and thought-provoking exercises to engage readers and help them develop their communication skills.

Whether you are a seasoned communicator looking to refine your abilities or someone just starting out on the path to better communication, this book is designed to meet your needs. It is a resource that will empower you to communicate with confidence, empathy, and authenticity, enabling you to connect with others, collaborate effectively, and make a positive impact in every area of your life.

Throughout history, communication has played a pivotal role in shaping societies, influencing cultures, and fostering understanding between individuals. From ancient cave paintings to the invention of the written word, from the telegraph to the internet, our methods of communication have evolved, but the core principles remain timeless.

In an era where technology has made communication instantaneous and global, we often find ourselves inundated with an overwhelming influx of messages, opinions, and voices. It is now more important than ever to discern meaningful communication from the noise and to foster genuine connections amidst the digital chaos.

This book is not just about the mechanics of communication, but also about the heart behind it. It emphasizes the importance of empathy, respect, and active listening as crucial ingredients for effective communication. It encourages readers to recognize the power of their words and the impact they can have on others. It invites us to step out of our comfort zones, embrace vulnerability, and strive for authentic connections.

As you embark on this communication journey, remember that the true essence of communication lies in fostering understanding, promoting harmony, and building bridges of empathy across diverse perspectives. Whether you are seeking to enhance your personal relationships, excel in your professional endeavours, or contribute to a world in need of better communication, this book will equip you with the knowledge and skills to do so.

I invite you to dive into the pages ahead, engage with the concepts presented, and apply them in your daily interactions. Let this be a transformative experience that not only improves your own communication skills but also inspires you to become an advocate for effective communication in your community.

Now, let us embark on this quest together, united by the belief in the power of communication. May this book be a guiding light on your path to becoming a masterful communicator, and may it empower you to make a lasting positive impact, one conversation at a time.

Here's to the journey of communication excellence!

**Sai Siddhanth Botta**

# Author's Note

Dear Readers,

Welcome to this journey into the world of communication! I am thrilled to have you join me as we explore the intricacies and nuances of effective communication together.

Before we begin, I wanted to express my sincere gratitude for your interest in this book. It is my hope that the ideas and insights shared within these pages will empower you to become a better communicator, foster stronger connections, and navigate the complexities of communication in today's world.

As an author, researcher, and practitioner of communication, I have witnessed firsthand the transformative power of effective communication. From personal relationships to professional success, the ability to communicate clearly, empathetically, and assertively can make all the difference in our lives.

Through research, real-life anecdotes, and practical exercises, I aim to provide you with a comprehensive toolkit to enhance your communication skills. But this book is more than just a collection of tips and techniques. It is a journey of self-discovery, growth, and transformation.

We will delve into various aspects of communication, such as active listening, nonverbal cues, conflict resolution, and the power of empathy. Together, we will explore how to navigate difficult conversations, overcome barriers, and build meaningful connections with others.

I want to emphasize that effective communication is not a one-size-fits-all approach. Each individual brings their unique experiences, backgrounds, and perspectives to the table. Therefore, I encourage you to adapt and customize the strategies presented in this book to suit your own communication style and context.

Throughout this journey, I invite you to reflect on your own communication habits, beliefs, and biases. Recognizing and challenging our own communication patterns is a crucial step towards personal growth and building stronger relationships.

Remember, this book is not meant to be a quick fix or a magic formula. It takes time, practice, and commitment to develop and improve our communication skills. So be patient with yourself, embrace the process, and celebrate even the smallest victories along the way.

I would love to hear about your own experiences and insights as you progress through this book. Feel free to share your thoughts, questions, and success stories with me. Together, we can create a supportive community of communicators who inspire and uplift one another.

Thank you once again for joining me on this communication journey. I am excited to see how these principles and strategies unfold in your life and relationships. Let us embark on this adventure together, armed with curiosity, empathy, and a determination to make a positive impact through effective communication.

Warmest Regards,
**Soujanya Pudi**

# Chapter 1

# Impact of Modernization on Professional Communication

The impact of modernization on professional communication has been significant, with technological advancements changing the way we communicate and interact in the workplace. In this book, we will explore how modernization has affected professional communication in various ways and the implications of these changes.

One of the most significant impacts of modernization on professional communication is the rise of digital communication tools. With the advent of email, instant messaging, video conferencing, and social media, professionals can conncct with colleagues, clients, and customers across the globe in real-time. This has made communication faster and more efficient, allowing organizations to streamline operations and improve productivity. Moreover, digital communication provides a record of conversations that can be easily referenced or searched, which helps in resolving disputes or misunderstandings that may arise.

However, the proliferation of digital communication also has its downsides. It has led to an increase in interruptions and distractions that can disrupt workflow, causing employees to lose focus and become less productive. Digital communication also has the potential to blur the lines between work and personal life, leading to burnout and stress among employees. Moreover, the impersonal nature of digital communication can lead to misunderstandings and conflicts, as tone and context are lost in translation.

Another impact of modernization on professional communication is the use of data analytics in decision-making. Organizations can now collect and analyze vast amounts of data about their customers, employees, and operations to gain insights into trends, patterns, and performance indicators. This can help organizations make informed decisions, optimize processes, and develop better strategies for growth. However, it also raises concerns about data privacy and the ethical use of data. The responsibility of handling sensitive information falls on organizations, and they must ensure that data is not misused, mishandled or leaked.

The rise of flexible work arrangements, such as remote work and telecommuting, is another impact of modernization on professional communication. These arrangements have become increasingly popular, facilitated by advances in technology that enable employees to work from anywhere in the world. Flexible work arrangements can enhance employee satisfaction, reduce commuting costs and improve work-life balance. However, they also pose a challenge for effective communication and collaboration. Remote workers are often isolated, leading to decreased engagement and integration with the team, which may ultimately affect productivity.

Modernization has affected the communication skills required to succeed in the workplace.

Today's professionals must be adept at using digital communication tools, such as email and social media, to communicate effectively.

However, they must also be skilled in face-to-face communication, active listening and collaboration to build strong relationships with colleagues and clients. The ability to communicate across cultures and languages is also becoming increasingly important as organizations become more globalized.

Modernization has had a significant impact on professional communication, changing the way we communicate and interact in the workplace. While it has brought many benefits, such as faster and more efficient communication, it has also created challenges, such as distractions and interruptions. As professionals, we must adapt to these changes and develop the skills needed to succeed in today's digital age while maintaining strong interpersonal relationships.

# Chapter 2

# Skill Gap Conundrum

The talent landscape is constantly evolving, presenting unique challenges for employers and employees alike. One of the most significant challenges facing the talent landscape today is the growing skill gap conundrum. The skill gap conundrum refers to the mismatch between the skills that employers require and the skills that workers possess. There are several reasons why this skill gap is growing, including new technology, changing demographics, and the global economy. In addition to the skill gap, there are other challenges across the talent landscape that are worth exploring.

The skill gap conundrum is a complex issue that requires a multifaceted approach to address. One factor contributing to the skill gap is the rapid pace of technological change. New technologies are emerging all the time, and many workers lack the skills needed to keep up with these changes. Moreover, the traditional education system may not be equipped to prepare workers for the new jobs that emerge from these technological advancements.

Another factor contributing to the skill gap is changing demographics. With an aging workforce, many industries are experiencing a shortage of skilled workers. Additionally, younger workers may not have the necessary skills or experience to fill these roles.

To address the skill gap conundrum, employers should invest in training and development programs that help workers acquire the skills they need to succeed in their jobs. Moreover, educational institutions should work closely with employers to ensure that their curriculum and training programs align with industry needs.

## Other Challenges

In addition to the skill gap conundrum, there are other challenges across the talent landscape that are worth exploring. One challenge is the increasing prevalence of the gig economy. Many workers today are self-employed or work on a freelance basis, which presents unique challenges for employers and workers alike.

In the gig economy, workers often lack the job security and benefits offered by traditional employment arrangements. Employers must also navigate the legal and regulatory landscape surrounding this type of work arrangement.

Another challenge facing the talent landscape is the growing demand for soft skills. While technical skills are still essential, many employers are placing a greater emphasis on soft skills, such as communication, critical thinking, and creativity. Moreover, globalization has made cross-cultural competency an increasingly important skill for workers to possess.

## Conclusion

The talent landscape is constantly evolving, presenting unique challenges for employers and employees alike. The skill gap conundrum is one of the most significant challenges facing the talent landscape today, along with other challenges such as the gig economy and the growing demand for soft skills. To address these challenges, employers must invest in training and development programs, and educational institutions must work closely with employers to ensure that their curriculum and training programs align with industry needs. By taking a multifaceted approach, we can ensure that workers have the skills and experience they need to succeed in the modern workforce.

# Chapter 3

# The Power of ASK-Attitude Skills & Knowledge

Unleashing the Potential Within

Attitude is a fundamental aspect of human behavior that influences our thoughts, emotions, and actions. It shapes our perceptions, determines our success in various life domains, and profoundly impacts our overall well-being. This essay explores the concept of attitude, its components, types, and the significant role it plays in personal and professional development.

Attitude, often described as a mental state or predisposition, reflects our underlying beliefs, opinions, and feelings towards people, events, situations, and objects. It is intangible yet powerful, acting as a lens through which we view the world. Attitude encompasses a wide range of emotions, including positivity, negativity, optimism, pessimism, and everything in between. This essay aims to delve into the nature of attitude, its impact on various aspects of life, and strategies for cultivating a positive and growth-oriented attitude.

## 1. Components of Attitude

Attitude consists of three primary components: cognitive, affective, and behavioral. The cognitive component refers to our thoughts, beliefs, and opinions about a particular subject. The affective component encompasses the emotional response associated with an attitude, influencing our feelings and sentiments. Lastly, the behavioral component involves our actions and behaviors that reflect our attitude towards a given situation or individual.

## 2. Types of Attitude

Attitudes can be classified into various categories based on their nature and focus. Positive attitudes, such as optimism, gratitude, and resilience, are characterized by a constructive and hopeful outlook towards life. Negative attitudes, on the other hand, include cynicism, pessimism, and resentment, which hinder personal growth and impede harmonious relationships. Attitudes can also be specific to certain areas, such as work-related attitudes or attitude towards societal issues.

## 3. The Impact of Attitude

Our attitude has far-reaching consequences on all aspects of life. In personal relationships, a positive attitude fosters empathy, understanding, and effective communication, while a negative attitude breeds conflict and misunderstanding. Professionally, individuals with a positive attitude are more likely to excel in their careers, demonstrate resilience, and inspire others. Attitude also plays a vital role in health and well-being, influencing stress levels, immune function, and overall quality of life.

## 4. Cultivating a Positive Attitude

Developing a positive attitude is a lifelong journey that requires self-awareness, introspection, and conscious effort. It involves challenging negative beliefs, reframing situations, practicing gratitude, adopting an open-minded approach, and surrounding oneself with positive influences. Techniques such as cognitive restructuring, mindfulness, and positive affirmations can aid in reshaping attitudes towards a more positive and growth-oriented mindset.

## 5. Overcoming Barriers to Attitude Change

Despite the importance of a positive attitude, individuals often face barriers to changing their attitudes.

These barriers can include deep-rooted biases, external influences, fear of change, and self-limiting beliefs. Overcoming these barriers requires self-reflection, seeking support from mentors or therapists, and consciously exposing oneself to new perspectives and experiences.

## 6. The Role of Education in Fostering Positive Attitudes

Education has a significant role to play in fostering positive attitudes. Schools and educational institutions should incorporate programs that teach emotional intelligence, empathy, and resilience, helping students develop healthy attitudes towards themselves and others. Teachers can serve as role models, fostering an inclusive and supportive classroom environment that encourages positive attitudes among students.

## 7. Conclusion

Attitude, with its cognitive, affective, and behavioral components, is a powerful force that shapes our thoughts, emotions, and actions. It influences how we navigate personal relationships, professional endeavors, and our overall well-being. By cultivating a positive attitude and overcoming barriers to change, we can unlock our true potential, fostering personal growth, success, and happiness. It is a lifelong journey, requiring continuous self-reflection, learning, and adaptation. Ultimately, our attitude determines how we perceive and respond to the world, making it a key determinant of our quality of life.

## SKILLS

Skills serve as the foundation of our abilities, enabling us to perform tasks, solve problems, and achieve goals. This essay explores the concept of skills, their importance in personal and professional development, and strategies for acquiring and enhancing them. It discusses the different types of skills, such as cognitive, technical, social, and emotional skills, and emphasizes the significance of continuous learning and practice to master these skills.

1. Skills are a crucial aspect of human potential, allowing individuals to effectively navigate through life's challenges and make meaningful contributions in various domains. From cognitive abilities to technical expertise and interpersonal competencies, skills shape our capabilities and determine our level of success. This essay aims to delve into the nature of skills, their significance, and strategies for acquiring and improving them.

2. Types of Skills

    2.1 Cognitive Skills: Cognitive skills refer to mental processes involved in acquiring knowledge, thinking critically, and problem-solving. These skills include logical reasoning, attention to detail, creativity, and analytical thinking. Developing cognitive skills enhances our ability to process information, make informed decisions, and adapt to new situations.

    2.2 Technical Skills: Technical skills are specific abilities related to a particular field or occupation. They involve practical knowledge and expertise required to perform specific tasks or operate certain tools or equipment. Examples of technical skills include programming, graphic design, carpentry, and engineering. Acquiring and honing technical skills is essential for professional success in specialized fields.

    2.3 Social Skills: Social skills encompass the ability to interact and communicate effectively with others. These skills involve active listening, empathy, conflict resolution, and persuasive communication. Strong social skills...

3. Emotional Skills: Emotional skills, also known as emotional intelligence, refer to the ability to understand and manage one's own emotions and

the emotions of others. These skills include self-awareness, empathy, emotional regulation, and effective communication. Developing emotional skills allows individuals to navigate social situations, build strong relationships, and promote collaboration and harmony in personal and professional settings.

4. The Importance of Skills Development

   Developing a diverse range of skills is essential for personal and professional growth. Here are some reasons why skills development is crucial:

4.1 Career Advancement: Acquiring and enhancing skills opens up new opportunities for career advancement. Employers value individuals with a versatile skill set, as it demonstrates adaptability and the ability to take on new challenges.

4.2 Problem-Solving Abilities: Skills like critical thinking, creativity, and analytical reasoning enable individuals to approach problems from different perspectives and develop innovative solutions.

4.3 Effective Communication: Strong communication skills, both verbal and written, are essential in various aspects of life, including personal relationships, teamwork, and leadership roles. Effective communication fosters understanding, resolves conflicts, and facilitates collaboration.

4.4 Adaptability and Resilience: In today's fast-paced world, the ability to adapt to changes and bounce back from setbacks is crucial. Developing skills such as flexibility, resilience, and problem-solving enables individuals to navigate uncertainties and thrive in dynamic environments.

5. Strategies for Skill Acquisition and Improvement

To acquire and improve skills, individuals can follow these strategies:

5.1 Set Clear Goals: Define the specific skills you want to acquire or enhance. Set SMART goals that are Specific, Measurable, Attainable, Relevant, and Time-bound.

5.2 Seek Learning Opportunities: Take advantage of various learning resources, such as books, online courses, workshops, and seminars. Engage in continuous learning and stay updated with the latest developments in your field of interest.

5.3 Practice Regularly: Skills need consistent practice to improve. Dedicate time each day or week to practice and refine your skills.

5.4 Seek Feedback: Feedback from mentors, peers, or experts can provide valuable insights into areas of improvement and help you refine your skills.

5.5 Collaborate and Network: Engage in collaborative projects, join professional communities, and network with like-minded individuals to learn from their experiences and gain exposure to new perspectives.

Skills play a vital role in personal and professional development, enabling individuals to tackle challenges, achieve goals, and thrive in various domains. By understanding the different types of skills, recognizing their importance, and implementing effective strategies for skill acquisition and improvement, individuals can unlock their full potential and enhance their chances of success in today's dynamic world. Remember, skills are not fixed, but instead, they can be developed and mastered with dedication, practice, and a growth mindset. So, embark on your journey to master skills and unleash your true potential.

Seek Learning Opportunities: Look for opportunities to learn and practice your desired skills. This can include enrolling in courses, attending workshops or seminars, joining online communities or forums, and seeking out mentors or experts in the field.

Practice Regularly: Consistent practice is key to skill development. Find ways to incorporate your chosen skill into your daily life or work. For example, if you want to improve your public speaking skills, seek opportunities to speak in front of an audience, such as volunteering for presentations or joining a public speaking club.

Receive Feedback: Feedback is crucial for skill improvement. Seek constructive feedback from mentors, peers, or trainers who can provide valuable insights and suggestions for improvement. Actively listen to feedback and make necessary adjustments to your approach.

Reflect and Evaluate: Regularly reflect on your progress and evaluate your skill development. Assess your strengths and areas for improvement, celebrate milestones, and set new goals to continue challenging yourself.

Stay Updated and Evolve: Skills are not static, and it's important to stay updated with advancements and changes in your chosen field. Stay curious, read books or articles, attend conferences, and participate in continuous learning to keep your skills relevant and adaptable.

## Overcoming Challenges in Skill Development

Developing skills can come with challenges. Here are some common obstacles and strategies to overcome them:

Time Management: Finding time for skill development can be challenging, especially alongside other responsibilities. Prioritize your goals, create a schedule, and allocate dedicated time for skill-building activities.

Perseverance: Developing skills takes time and effort. Stay committed to your goals, even when faced with setbacks or slow progress. Stay motivated and remind yourself of the long-term benefits and rewards of skill development.

Fear of Failure: Fear of failure can hinder skill development. Embrace a growth mindset and view failures as learning opportunities. Take risks, learn from mistakes, and keep pushing yourself outside of your comfort zone.

Lack of Resources: Limited access to resources or opportunities can be a challenge. Look for free or low-cost alternatives, utilize online platforms or communities, and network with others in your field to find mentorship or collaborative opportunities.

Remember, skill development is a lifelong process. Embrace curiosity, persistence, and a growth mindset to continually enhance your skills and broaden your horizons. With dedication and consistent effort, you can achieve personal and professional success through skill development.

## KNOWLEDGE

Knowledge is crucial for effective communication in various ways:

1. Clarity and Accuracy: Having knowledge about the subject matter allows you to communicate your ideas, thoughts, and information clearly and accurately. When you possess knowledge, you can use appropriate terminology, provide relevant details, and present your points in a logical and organized manner. This ensures that your e-communication is coherent and easily understood by the recipient.
2. Credibility and Trust: Knowledge builds credibility and trust in your e-communication. When you demonstrate expertise in your area of knowledge, it establishes you as a reliable source of information. This helps to gain the trust of your audience and ensures that your e-communications are taken seriously and valued.

3. Effective Problem Solving: Knowledge equips you with the necessary tools to identify and solve problems efficiently through e-communication. When you understand the subject matter, you can anticipate potential challenges, propose practical solutions, and provide accurate guidance to others. This enhances your ability to communicate effectively in dealing with issues or providing support remotely.

4. Adaptability and Flexibility: In the digital world, new technologies and platforms emerge regularly, requiring individuals to adapt and learn new skills to communicate effectively. Having knowledge about emerging trends, tools, and practices enables you to stay up-to-date and harness the potential of new communication channels. It allows you to tailor your e-communication strategies to specific platforms and contexts, ensuring your messages reach the intended recipients effectively.

5. Audience Engagement: Knowledge enables you to understand your target audience and tailor your e-communication accordingly. When you have insights into their needs, preferences, and communication styles, you can create content that engages and resonates with them. This leads to better communication outcomes,

increased interaction, and stronger connections with your audience.

Overall, knowledge is essential for effective e-communication as it provides clarity, credibility, problem-solving abilities, adaptability, and audience engagement. By harnessing your knowledge effectively, you can communicate more effectively and achieve your communication goals in the digital realm.

Acquiring knowledge through social interactions plays a vital role in its application across various domains. Here are a few ways in which social interactions enhance the application of knowledge:

1. Collaboration and Shared Learning: Social interactions enable individuals to collaborate, share ideas, and learn from each other's experiences. Through discussion, debates, and group projects, individuals can gain new perspectives and insights that they might not have encountered independently. This collaborative learning process enhances the depth and breadth of knowledge, making it more applicable in different domains.
2. Networking and Access to Resources: Social interactions provide opportunities for networking, connecting with experts, and accessing valuable resources. By engaging with

individuals who have expertise in specific fields, one can tap into their knowledge base, gain practical insights, and get access to relevant research, tools, or equipment. This facilitates the application of knowledge in a more effective and targeted manner.

3. Validation and Feedback: Social interactions allow for the validation and evaluation of knowledge. Discussions with peers, mentors, or experts help in refining ideas, identifying gaps in understanding, and receiving constructive feedback. This feedback loop is essential in enhancing the application of knowledge by addressing any misconceptions, improving methods, and ensuring accuracy.

4. Cultural and Contextual Understanding: Social interactions expose individuals to diverse perspectives, cultures, and contexts. This exposure helps in broadening one's understanding of how knowledge is applied in different situations. By engaging with people from different backgrounds, individuals can gain a nuanced understanding of how knowledge is shaped by cultural, social, and historical factors. This understanding enhances the application of knowledge by adapting it to specific contexts and fostering inclusivity.

5. Emotional Intelligence and Interpersonal Skills: Social interactions contribute to the development of emotional intelligence and interpersonal skills, which are crucial for effective knowledge application. By engaging in conversations, active listening, empathy, and collaboration, individuals can navigate complex social dynamics, build relationships, and communicate their knowledge effectively. These skills facilitate the application of knowledge in domains where interaction and communication are key, such as leadership, teamwork, and customer relations.

In summary, acquiring knowledge through social interactions enables collaboration, networking, feedback, cultural understanding, and the development of interpersonal skills. These factors collectively enhance the application of knowledge by broadening perspectives, accessing resources, validating ideas, adapting knowledge to specific contexts, and facilitating effective communication.

# Chapter 4
# Personality Development

Personality development refers to the process of enhancing and improving various aspects of one's personality. It involves acquiring and developing qualities, skills, attitudes, and behaviors that contribute to personal growth, self-confidence, effective communication, and overall success in life.

Here are some key tips for personality development:

Take the time to understand your strengths, weaknesses, values, and goals. This self-reflection allows you to identify areas for improvement and set personal development goals. Engage in lifelong learning to broaden your knowledge and skills. Read books, attend workshops, take courses, and seek out opportunities for personal and professional growth.

Positive mindset: Cultivate a positive attitude and outlook on life. Practice gratitude, optimism, and kindness towards yourself and others. Surround yourself with positive influences and avoid negative self-talk. Effective communication: Develop strong communication skills, both verbal and non-verbal. Practice active listening, clarity in expression, and empathy in your interactions with others. Emotional intelligence: Enhance your emotional intelligence by understanding and managing your own emotions, as well as empathizing with others. This skill helps build better relationships and enables effective conflict resolution. Time management: Learn to prioritize tasks, set realistic goals, and manage your time effectively. This skill allows you to be more productive, reduce stress, and achieve a better work-life balance. Confidence building: Work on building self-confidence and self-esteem. Celebrate your achievements, step out of your comfort zone, and take on new challenges to boost your confidence levels. Adaptability and resilience: Develop the ability to adapt to change and bounce back from setbacks. Embrace challenges as opportunities for growth and learn from failures. Interpersonal skills: Enhance your social skills, such as teamwork, leadership, and collaboration. Build strong relationships, network with others, and develop effective interpersonal communication. Personal grooming: Pay attention to your physical appearance, hygiene, and personal style. Dress appropriately for different occasions and present yourself in a professional manner.

Remember, personality development is a lifelong journey. It requires consistent effort, self-reflection, and a willingness to grow and improve. Embrace the process, be patient with yourself, and enjoy the rewards of personal growth and development.

Self-awareness is a crucial aspect of personal growth and overall success in life. Here are a few ways self-awareness can contribute to your development:

Identifying strengths and weaknesses: Self-awareness allows you to recognize your strengths, which can be cultivated and leveraged to achieve your goals. It also helps you acknowledge your weaknesses, giving you the opportunity to work on them and improve.

Setting realistic goals: By understanding your abilities, limitations, and values, self-awareness enables you to set realistic and meaningful goals. This helps direct your efforts and resources towards activities that align with your aspirations and give you a sense of purpose.

Improved decision-making: Being self-aware enhances your ability to make effective decisions. When you understand your values, priorities, and goals, you can evaluate options more objectively and make choices that align with your long-term vision.

Building better relationships: Self-awareness helps you understand your emotions, reactions, and communication style. This awareness translates into better interpersonal skills as you become more attuned to the needs and feelings of others. It also allows you to manage conflicts more effectively and build deeper, more authentic connections with people.

Increased self-confidence: Self-awareness brings clarity about who you are and what you stand for. This knowledge fosters self-confidence because you have a strong understanding of your abilities, values, and boundaries. This confidence radiates in your actions and interactions with others, leading to greater success in various areas of life.

Enhancing emotional intelligence: Self-awareness is a cornerstone of emotional intelligence. It helps you recognize and understand your emotions, as well as how they influence your thoughts and behaviors. This awareness enables you to regulate your emotions effectively, handle stress, and empathize with others, all of which contribute to healthier relationships and personal growth.

Continuous self-improvement: Self-awareness fuels a desire for self-improvement and ongoing personal development. It motivates you to seek feedback, learn from your experiences, and continuously strive for growth. With a growth mindset fostered by self-awareness, you have Increased resilience: Self-awareness allows you to identify and understand your triggers, stressors, and patterns of behavior. With this awareness, you can develop coping strategies and resilience to navigate challenges and setbacks effectively. You become more adaptable and better equipped to bounce back from difficult situations.

Personal growth and self-improvement: Self-awareness is the foundation for personal growth and self-improvement. By understanding your strengths and weaknesses, you can focus on areas that need improvement and work towards becoming the best version of yourself. This continuous self-reflection and growth contribute to a more fulfilling and meaningful life.

Better self-care: When you are self-aware, you have a deeper understanding of your needs, both physically and mentally. This enables you to prioritize self-care and make choices that support your well-being. You are more likely to engage in activities that bring you joy, nurture your body, and cultivate a positive mindset.

Effective leadership: Self-awareness is a key trait of effective leaders. When you are aware of your own strengths, weaknesses, and emotions, you can lead with authenticity and empathy. You are also more open to feedback and can make necessary adjustments to improve your leadership style. Developing self-awareness takes time and ongoing effort. It involves practices like self-reflection, introspection, mindfulness, and seeking feedback from others. By cultivating self-awareness, you can unlock your full potential, build meaningful relationships, and lead a more fulfilled life. Developing self-awareness can indeed help individuals navigate challenges and setbacks more effectively.

Identifying triggers and patterns: Self-awareness allows you to identify your triggers, the things that cause stress or emotional reactions. By understanding what triggers you, you can better prepare for challenging situations and develop strategies to manage your emotions effectively. Additionally, self-awareness helps you recognize patterns of behavior or negative thoughts that may contribute to setbacks. This awareness allows you to break free from those patterns and make positive changes. Taking responsibility: Self-awareness empowers you to take responsibility for your actions, choices, and outcomes. Instead of blaming external factors, you recognize the role you play in creating your reality. This mindset shift enables you to focus on finding solutions rather than dwelling on the problem. It promotes a proactive approach to challenges, leading to quicker and more effective problem-solving. Adapting and adjusting: With self-awareness, you gain insights into your strengths, weaknesses, and limitations. This understanding helps you adapt and adjust your approach when faced with obstacles or setbacks. You can leverage your strengths to find alternative solutions or seek support in areas where you may need assistance. Being aware of your limitations allows you to be realistic in your expectations and seek help when necessary. Building resilience: Self-awareness contributes to building resilience, the ability to bounce back from challenges. When you are self-aware, you can recognize and manage your emotions during difficult times. You become more mindful, developing coping strategies such as practicing self-care, seeking support from others, or engaging in activities that bring you joy. This resilience helps you navigate setbacks with a more positive mindset and bounce back stronger than before. Learning from experiences: Self-awareness enables you to reflect on your experiences and learn from them. By analyzing what went well and what didn't, you can extract valuable lessons for future challenges. This introspective process allows you to grow and make improvements, making you better prepared to handle similar situations in the future.

Overall, developing self-awareness provides individuals with the tools to understand themselves better, manage their emotions effectively, and make conscious choices during challenging times. It empowers them to take control of their lives and navigate setbacks with resilience and adaptability. Learning and growth: Self-awareness promotes a growth mindset, where setbacks and challenges are seen as opportunities for learning and personal development. By being aware of your strengths and weaknesses, you can focus on areas that need improvement and actively seek opportunities for growth. You can engage in continuous learning, acquire new skills, and adapt to changing circumstances more effectively.

Self-awareness enhances your communication skills. When you are aware of your emotions, thoughts, and reactions, you can express yourself more clearly and assertively. You can also recognize when your emotions might be affecting your communication and take steps to address them before engaging in conversations. Being aware of your own communication style can also help you better understand and empathize with others, improving your relationships and collaboration during challenging times.

Building meaningful relationships: Self-awareness allows you to understand your values, needs, and boundaries, which are essential in building healthy and meaningful relationships. It helps you navigate difficult conversations or conflicts by expressing yourself authentically without compromising your values. Moreover, self-awareness allows you to recognize and appreciate the unique perspectives and emotions of others, fostering empathy and connection.

Decision-making: Self-awareness plays a crucial role in making sound decisions during setbacks. By understanding your emotions, biases, and core values, you can make decisions that align with your long-term goals and well-being. Self-awareness helps you separate your emotional reactions from objective analysis, enabling you to make rational choices even in challenging situations. Resolving inner conflicts: Setbacks and challenges often give rise to inner conflicts, such as doubts, fears, or conflicting priorities. Self-awareness helps you identify and resolve these internal conflicts by understanding your motivations, values, and desires. This self-reflection empowers you to make choices that align with your true self and minimize inner turmoil.

Overall, developing self-awareness is a valuable tool for navigating challenges and setbacks. It allows you to understand yourself better, manage your emotions effectively, and make informed decisions that lead to personal growth and resilience.

# Chapter 5
# Self-care & Communication

Self-care is an important aspect of maintaining overall well-being and managing the challenges and setbacks life throws our way. It involves taking intentional actions to nurture your physical, mental, and emotional health. Here are some key areas of self-care:

Physical self-care: This involves taking care of your body through activities such as regular exercise, eating healthy, getting enough sleep, and practicing good hygiene. Paying attention to your physical needs allows you to have more energy, better focus, and improved overall health.

Emotional self-care: Emotional self-care involves recognizing and acknowledging your feelings, and taking steps to nurture your emotional well-being. This can include activities such as journaling, seeking support from loved ones, engaging in activities that bring you joy, practicing mindfulness or meditation, and creating healthy boundaries.

Mental self-care: This encompasses activities that support your mental well-being and cognitive function. It can involve engaging in activities that stimulate your mind, such as reading, learning new skills, participating in puzzles or brain games, and practicing relaxation techniques like deep breathing or meditation.

Social self-care: Humans are social creatures, and nurturing connections with others is vital for our well-being. Engaging in social self-care can involve spending quality time with loved ones, joining communities or groups with shared interests, and seeking support or guidance from trusted individuals.

Spiritual self-care: This area focuses on nourishing your spiritual beliefs and connecting with something larger than yourself. For some, it may involve religious activities, while for others, it could be spending time in nature, practicing meditation or mindfulness, or engaging in activities that align with their values and personal growth.

Remember, self-care is highly individualized, and what works for one person may not work for another. It's important to listen to your own needs and preferences and find practices that resonate with you. Incorporating self-care into your routine can help you better cope with setbacks, reduce stress, and improve your overall well-being.

Regular exercise and healthy eating play crucial roles in improving overall well-being. Here's how they contribute:

Physical health: Regular exercise helps maintain a healthy weight, reduces the risk of chronic diseases (such as heart disease, diabetes, and certain cancers), strengthens muscles and bones, improves cardiovascular health, and enhances overall physical fitness. Healthy eating provides the body with essential nutrients, vitamins, and minerals needed for optimal functioning, supports a strong immune system, aids in digestion, and helps maintain a healthy body composition.

Mental health: Exercise has been shown to boost mood by increasing the production of endorphins, which are natural mood elevators. It also reduces symptoms of depression and anxiety, improves cognitive function, enhances sleep quality, and increases self-esteem and body image. Healthy eating, especially a diet rich in fruits, vegetables, whole grains, and omega-3 fatty acids, is associated with lower rates of mental health disorders and improved cognitive function.

Energy and vitality: Regular exercise improves energy levels by increasing blood flow and oxygen delivery to the muscles and other tissues. It also helps improve sleep quality, which in turn enhances daytime energy levels. Healthy eating provides the body with the necessary macronutrients and micronutrients that fuel cellular processes, support energy metabolism, and promote vitality.

Stress management: Exercise is a natural stress reliever. It helps reduce cortisol levels (the stress hormone) and stimulates the production of endorphins, which can elevate mood and promote relaxation. Healthy eating contributes to stress management by providing the nutrients needed for optimal brain function and regulating blood sugar levels, which can affect mood and stress levels.

Longevity and overall quality of life: Regular exercise and healthy eating are associated with a reduced risk of premature death and an improved quality of life. They help prevent and manage chronic diseases, enhance physical functioning, maintain cognitive health, boost immunity, and promote overall well-being.

Incorporating regular exercise and healthy eating habits into your lifestyle can have profound effects on your physical and mental well-being, leading to improved overall quality of life.

## Skill versus knowledge

Skill and knowledge are two distinct but interconnected concepts.

Knowledge refers to the understanding, information, and awareness that a person possesses about a particular subject or area. It is acquired through learning, education, training, and experience. Knowledge can be theoretical or practical and can be obtained from various sources such as books, teachers, research, and personal exploration.

Skill, on the other hand, refers to the ability to perform specific tasks or activities effectively. It is developed through practice, repetition, and hands-on experience. Skills are more focused on application and performance rather than simply having knowledge about something. Skills require practical proficiency, dexterity, and the ability to execute tasks with precision and efficiency.

While knowledge provides the foundation and understanding of a subject, skill is the practical application of that knowledge. You can have extensive knowledge about a particular field or topic, but without the corresponding skills, you may not be able to effectively apply that knowledge in real-life situations.

For example, you may have extensive knowledge of programming languages, but unless you have the skill to write code and develop software, your knowledge alone may not be enough to be considered a skilled programmer.

In summary, knowledge is the theoretical understanding of a subject, while skill is the practical ability to perform tasks related to that subject. Both knowledge and skill are important and complement each other, as having knowledge enables the development of skills, and skills require a foundation of knowledge to be effectively applied.

One example of a profession or field where extensive knowledge is essential, but skill is not as important could be academia, particularly in research-based positions. In academia, researchers and scholars often focus on acquiring in-depth knowledge in their respective fields of study. They spend significant time studying, analyzing data, conducting experiments, and publishing papers to contribute to the body of knowledge in their area of expertise.

While researchers do need certain skills to carry out their work effectively, such as critical thinking, data analysis, and writing skills, the emphasis is more on knowledge acquisition and intellectual contributions. The ability to think critically, conduct thorough literature reviews, and generate new knowledge through research is often more valued in academia compared to certain practical skills.

However, it is important to note that even in academia, having certain skills can greatly enhance one's effectiveness and impact. For example, presentation skills can help researchers effectively communicate their findings, teaching skills can help them impart knowledge to students, and collaboration skills can facilitate interdisciplinary research projects.

Overall, while there are fields where extensive knowledge is crucial and skills may take a backseat, it is often the combination of both knowledge and skills that leads to success and excellence in any profession.

# Chapter 6
# Twentieth Century Skills

Twentieth-century skills, also known as 21st-century skills, refer to a set of competencies and abilities that are considered essential for individuals to thrive in the modern world. These skills are often seen as necessary for success in the digital age and in an increasingly interconnected and globalized society. Some examples of Twentieth-century skills include:

Critical thinking and problem-solving: The ability to analyze information, evaluate different perspectives, and find innovative solutions to complex problems.

Creativity and innovation: The capacity to think creatively, generate new ideas, and approach challenges with originality and flexibility.

Communication and collaboration: The skill to effectively express ideas, listen actively, and work collaboratively with diverse teams to achieve common goals.

Information literacy: The ability to identify, evaluate, and effectively use information from various sources, including digital media, while being aware of its credibility, relevance, and ethical use.

Digital literacy: The competence to navigate and utilize digital technologies, including computer literacy, online communication, digital content creation, and data analysis.

Global and cultural awareness: The understanding and appreciation of diverse cultures, perspectives, and global issues, along with the ability to communicate across cultural boundaries.

Adaptability and resilience: The capacity to adapt to changing circumstances, learn from failures, and bounce back from setbacks.

Emotional intelligence: The ability to recognize and manage one's own emotions, as well as understand and empathize with others' emotions, leading to effective interpersonal relationships.

Leadership and teamwork: The capability to lead and inspire others, delegate tasks, and collaborate effectively within a team.

Lifelong learning: The mindset and motivation to continuously learn, acquire new knowledge, and develop new skills throughout one's life.

These Twentieth-century skills are considered critical for individuals to thrive in a rapidly evolving world, where technology, globalization, and the need for innovative thinking and problem-solving are increasingly important in various personal, academic, and professional contexts.

Developing and enhancing critical thinking and problem-solving skills requires practice and intentional effort. Here are some strategies you can use to strengthen these skills:

Ask Questions: Encourage curiosity by asking questions about the information you come across. Ask yourself why, how, and what if, to deepen your understanding and challenge assumptions.

Analyze Information: Learn to evaluate information critically. Look for evidence, assess credibility, and consider different perspectives and biases. Separate facts from opinions and examine underlying assumptions.

Seek Different Perspectives: Engage in discussions with people who have diverse viewpoints. This can help you gain new insights and challenge your own thinking.

Solve Real-Life Problems: Look for opportunities to apply critical thinking and problem-solving skills in your everyday life. Break problems down into smaller parts, analyze each part, and explore different possible solutions.

Practice Reflection: Regularly reflect on your own thinking processes and decisions. Consider what worked well and what could have been done differently. Reflecting on past experiences helps to improve problem-solving abilities Learn from Mistakes: Embrace failures as learning opportunities. When faced with challenges or setbacks, analyze what went wrong and identify areas for improvement.

Develop Analytical Skills: Read books, articles, and research papers that challenge your thinking. Practice analyzing arguments and identifying logical fallacies.

Use Technology Wisely: Utilize online resources, educational platforms, and tools that promote critical thinking and problem-solving skills. For example, online puzzles, brain teasers, and strategy games can help sharpen your cognitive abilities.

Collaborate with Others: Engage in group projects or team activities where you can brainstorm ideas, seek feedback, and work together to solve problems. Collaborative environments promote diverse thinking and creative problem-solving.

Continuous Learning: Cultivate a growth mindset and have a thirst for knowledge. Stay open to learning new things, exploring different disciplines, and seeking out opportunities for personal and professional development.

Remember, developing critical thinking and problem-solving skills is an ongoing process. By consciously practicing these strategies, you can enhance your ability to think critically and approach problems with a more analytical and creative mindset.

# Chapter 7

# The Influence of Mother Tongue on Learning New Languages

The influence of mother tongue on learning new languages has been a topic of interest in the field of second language acquisition for decades. While some researchers argue that mother tongue can be a helpful tool in acquiring a new language, others suggest that it could be a hindrance. This essay will discuss the ways in which mother tongue influences the learning of new languages.

Firstly, mother tongue has a significant impact on the phonological development of an individual. The sounds of a language that a person is exposed to as an infant are stored in their brain and become part of their language system. As a result, when individuals learn a new language, they tend to transfer the sounds of their mother tongue onto the new language, which can lead to pronunciation errors. For example, an English speaker learning French may struggle to pronounce the French "r" sound as it does not exist in English. This difficulty arises since the English speaker transfers the English "r" sound into French, instead of learning the correct French pronunciation.

Secondly, mother tongue also affects the syntax and grammatical structures of a new language. The way we construct sentences and express ideas is influenced by our first language. This means that when we learn a new language, we have a tendency to transfer the grammar of our mother tongue onto the new language. For example, a Mandarin speaker learning English may struggle with using articles such as "a", "an", and "the" correctly. This is because Mandarin does not have these articles. As a result, the Mandarin speaker may omit them or use them incorrectly.

Thirdly, the vocabulary knowledge of an individual's mother tongue can also be beneficial in learning a new language. If two languages share similar vocabulary, it becomes easier for individuals to acquire the new language. For example, Spanish and Italian share many cognates, which are words that have the same or similar meanings in both languages. This makes it easier for someone who speaks Spanish to learn Italian.

Another way mother tongue can be beneficial in learning a new language is through transfer. Transfer refers to when a person applies knowledge from their first language to help them learn a second language. For example, a person who speaks French and is learning Spanish may use their knowledge of French verb conjugation to help them learn Spanish verb conjugation since the two languages share many similarities in this area.

On the other hand, mother tongue can also be a hindrance in learning a new language. One way is through interference. Interference refers to when the rules and structures of one language affect the acquisition of another language. For example, a German speaker learning English may struggle with using the correct word order as German syntax is different from English syntax.

Another way in which mother tongue can be a hindrance is through fossilization. Fossilization occurs when an individual reaches a plateau in their language development and does not progress beyond a certain level. This can happen if the rules of the mother tongue become so ingrained that thcy cannot be unlearned, even when they conflict with the rules of the new language.

In conclusion, the influence of mother tongue on learning a new language is complex. While it can be a helpful tool in some instances, it can also be a hindrance. Phonological, syntactic, and lexical differences between languages can impact new language acquisition. However, transfer, similarity in vocabulary and grammatical structures between two languages can also facilitate the learning process. To learn a new language successfully, learners must develop an awareness of both similarities and differences between their mother tongue and the new language.

MTI stands for "Mother Tongue Influence". It refers to the influence of a person's mother tongue, or native language, on their pronunciation, intonation, and grammar when speaking a second or foreign language.

In business communication, MTI can have a significant impact on how messages are received and perceived by the audience. For example, if an individual has a strong MTI, it may make it difficult for them to convey their message clearly and effectively in a language other than their mother tongue. This can lead to misunderstandings, misinterpretations, or even negative impressions, which can ultimately affect the success of business deals, negotiations, or relationships.

Moreover, as business becomes increasingly globalized, there is an increasing demand for multilingual communication skills. In order to communicate effectively across languages and cultures, it is essential to minimize MTI. This can be achieved through training programs, language courses, and pronunciation exercises that help individuals develop a more neutral accent. By doing so, they will be able to convey their message more clearly, build rapport with their colleagues and clients, and ultimately achieve better business outcomes.

In conclusion, MTI can have a significant impact on business communication, and it is important for individuals to develop their multilingual skills and reduce their MTI to succeed in today's globalized business world.

MTI stands for "Mother Tongue Influence". It refers to the influence of a person's mother tongue, or native language, on their pronunciation, intonation, and grammar when speaking a second or foreign language.

In business communication, MTI can have a significant impact on how messages are received and perceived by the audience. For example, if an individual has a strong MTI, it may make it difficult for them to convey their message clearly and effectively in a language other than their mother tongue. This can lead to misunderstandings, misinterpretations, or even negative impressions, which can ultimately affect the success of business deals, negotiations, or relationships.

Moreover, as business becomes increasingly globalized, there is an increasing demand for multilingual communication skills. In order to communicate effectively across languages and cultures, it is essential to minimize MTI. This can be achieved through training programs, language courses, and pronunciation exercises that help individuals develop a more neutral accent. By doing so, they will be able to convey their message more clearly, build rapport with their colleagues and clients, and ultimately achieve better business outcomes.

In conclusion, MTI can have a significant impact on business communication, and it is important for individuals to develop their multilingual skills and reduce their MTI to succeed in today's globalized business world.

# Chapter 8

# Power Up Your Negotiation

Social media has also emerged as a powerful tool for businesses to engage with their customers and promote their products and services. Through targeted advertising and influencer marketing, companies can reach out to their audiences in ways that were not possible before. Yes, social media has revolutionized the way people communicate and interact with each other. Platforms like Facebook, Twitter, Instagram, and LinkedIn have become integral parts of our daily lives, enabling us to connect with friends, family, and colleagues across the globe.

However, social media communication also poses several challenges. The ease with which information can be shared on these platforms has led to the proliferation of fake news and misinformation, leading to a decline in trust in traditional media sources.

Additionally, the anonymity provided by social media can lead to the spread of hate speech and cyberbullying, affecting the mental health and well-being of users. Therefore, it is essential to cultivate responsible social media usage and promote digital literacy skills that equip individuals with the ability to navigate through the complexities of online communication

Negotiations are critical to success in many areas of life, from business to personal relationships. The ability to negotiate effectively can help individuals achieve their goals, resolve conflicts, and build stronger relationships with others. This essay explores the essential role of negotiation skills in achieving success and offers practical tips for honing these skills.

Firstly, negotiation skills are essential in business and professional settings. In today's globalized economy, negotiations are an integral part of business operations. Whether it is negotiating with suppliers, partners, or clients, businesses rely heavily on negotiation skills to secure favorable deals and achieve long-term success.

Effective negotiation skills help individuals to communicate their needs, interests, and concerns clearly to the other party. Additionally, negotiation skills enable individuals to find common ground and identify mutually beneficial solutions in complex situations. These skills can also help individuals to navigate potential conflicts, resolve disputes, and maintain positive relationships with colleagues, clients, and stakeholders.

Furthermore, negotiation skills are equally important in personal relationships. Whether it is negotiating household chores with a partner, resolving a disagreement with a friend, or bargaining with a street vendor, negotiation skills can help individuals to assert their needs while respecting the concerns of others.

In personal relationships, effective negotiation skills can promote healthy communication, build trust, and strengthen the bonds between individuals. On the other hand, a lack of negotiation skills can lead to misunderstandings, resentment, and strained relationships.

In addition to business and personal relationships, negotiation skills are also critical in social and political contexts. Leaders who possess strong negotiation skills can effectively represent the interests of their constituents, forge alliances with other leaders, and work towards achieving shared goals.

Furthermore, negotiation skills are critical to resolving conflicts peacefully and promoting social justice. Negotiation skills can be used to mediate disputes, broker peace agreements, and prevent violent conflicts. In these scenarios, effective negotiation skills can save lives and prevent the loss of valuable resources.

Thus, it is clear that negotiation skills are essential for success in many areas of life. Individuals who possess strong negotiation skills are better equipped to achieve their goals, resolve conflicts, and build positive relationships with others.

Now, let's examine some practical tips for honing your negotiation skills:

1. Prepare thoroughly: Before entering into a negotiation, it is essential to prepare thoroughly by researching the other party's interests, needs, and bargaining position. Additionally, individuals should prepare themselves by identifying their own interests and goals and developing a clear understanding of their "walk-away" point.
2. Listen actively: Active listening is a critical component of effective negotiation. By listening carefully to the other party's needs and concerns, negotiators can identify areas of common ground and find mutually agreeable solutions.
3. Communicate clearly: Effective communication is key to successful negotiations. Negotiators

should communicate their interests, needs, and concerns clearly and concisely, using language that is easy to understand. Additionally, negotiators should avoid defensive or confrontational language, which can derail negotiations and harm relationships.

4. Find common ground: The most successful negotiations are ones where both parties feel like they have gained something. Thus, negotiators should strive to find areas of common ground and develop mutually beneficial solutions that meet the needs of both parties.

5. Be creative: Effective negotiators are often creative problem-solvers who think outside the box. By approaching negotiations with an open mind and an eye for creative solutions, negotiators can find innovative ways to overcome obstacles and achieve their goals.

Negotiation skills are essential for success in today's world. Whether in business, personal relationships, or social and political contexts, negotiations are a critical aspect of achieving one's goals and building positive relationships with others. By honing their negotiation skills through careful preparation, active listening, clear communication, finding common ground, and creative problem-solving, individuals can enhance their chances of success in all areas of life.

# Chapter 9
# Netiquette

Netiquette, short for 'network etiquette,' is a code of conduct that governs online behavior. It encompasses the rules and guidelines that dictate how individuals should interact with one another online. The advent of the internet and social media has made communication more accessible and convenient, but it has also given rise to a new set of challenges relating to how people conduct themselves online. Netiquette is essential for maintaining respectful and productive online communication.

## Online Communication

Online communication is a ubiquitous part of modern-day communication. Social media platforms, chat rooms, discussion forums, and emails are just a few examples of how people communicate online. One of the most significant benefits of online communication is that it allows people to connect with others from all over the world. However, there are also drawbacks associated with online communication. For example, online communication often lacks the nuance and context that we find in face-to-face communication. This can lead to misunderstandings, misinterpretations, and conflict if not handled correctly.

## Netiquette Guidelines

The following are some essential netiquette guidelines that individuals should follow while engaging in online communication:

1. Be Respectful: Online interactions should be conducted with respect for others. Avoid derogatory language, personal attacks, and aggressive behavior. Always assume the best intentions of others and refrain from making assumptions about their motives or beliefs.

2. Be Clear: Online communication can often be misunderstood, so it's important to be clear and accurate in your messaging. Always proofread your messages and make sure they convey precisely what you intend to say.

3. Use Appropriate Language: Avoid using inappropriate language or profanity in your communication. This is especially important

when communicating with individuals, you don't know well.

4. Keep it Short and Simple: Online communication is often fast-paced, so it's essential to keep your messages short and to the point. Avoid using long, rambling sentences or paragraphs that can be challenging to follow.

5. Be Timely: Respond to messages promptly, particularly those from colleagues or customers. This shows that you value their time and are dedicated to providing excellent customer service.

6. Use Emojis and Acronyms Sparingly: While emojis and acronyms can be a helpful way to convey emotion or shorthand messages, they can also be misinterpreted. Use them sparingly and only when appropriate.

7. Be Mindful of Tone and Context: Without face-to-face interaction, it can be difficult to understand the context and tone of a message fully. Ensure that your communication conveys the appropriate tone and context.

## Conclusion

Netiquette is crucial for maintaining respectful and productive online communication. By following these guidelines, individuals can ensure that their online interactions are polite, clear, and accurate. Netiquette is also essential for maintaining trust and credibility, especially in professional situations where communication is critical. Practicing netiquette can help individuals build stronger relationships online and improve their overall online communication skills.

Digital etiquette, also known as netiquette, is a set of guidelines and rules that users of the internet and social media platforms follow while communicating and interacting with others online. Digital etiquette has become increasingly important as our lives become more dependent on technology and as we spend more time communicating online. The following essay will explore why digital etiquette is essential, the impact of poor digital etiquette, and the essential rules to follow for good digital manners.

## The Importance of Digital Etiquette

With the surge of social media platforms, messaging services, and online communities, communication has undergone significant changes in recent years. The ability to communicate with others instantaneously and globally has opened up a world of opportunity, but it has also introduced many challenges. As we continue to communicate more through text, email, and social media platforms, the way we interact has become more important than ever. It is now necessary to cultivate positive relationships with individuals and communities online, as our online presence has become nearly as important as our offline presence. Digital etiquette is crucial in helping us navigate this new world of communication.

## The Impact of Poor Digital Etiquette

Poor digital etiquette can have significant impacts and consequences such as negative emotions, miscommunications, and in severe cases, social isolation. Being impolite, insulting others, or being unresponsive can cause frustration or even anxiety in others, which can negatively impact relationships, collaborations, or everyday interactions. Poor digital etiquette can also create confusion and misunderstandings, leading to miscommunications and the spread of misinformation. Moreover, lack of digital etiquette can lead to social isolation as people may choose to disengage from online communities or even avoid communicating online entirely to avoid interactions that make them uncomfortable.

## Rules to Follow For Good Digital Manners

To avoid negative consequences, individuals who communicate and interact online should follow some general rules of digital etiquette. Some of these rules are outlined as follows.

1. Use Appropriate Tone and Language: The tone and language used in online communication should be professional or friendly, depending on the context. Always be careful about the tone you take when communicating online and avoid the use of offensive language. Utilize emojis or other informal communicational options when talking to people you have an informal relationship with.

2. Respect Others' Opinions: Digital communication through social media is a two-way street, which entails recognizing that everyone online is an individual, whether they agree with us or not. When we appreciate and accept various opinions and views, we build open-mindedness and increase the likelihood of constructive interaction.

3. Practice Safe Online Behaviors: Digital etiquette includes ensuring online safety practices such as safeguarding your personal identifiable information. Avoid sharing your personal identification details like your full official name, phone number, email, or residential address

or passcode to prevent falling victim to online fraud, identity theft.

4. Give constructive criticism or feedback: Always aim to provide constructive feedback and criticism. Your comments should educate and raise awareness, not insult or discourage the recipient. Be specific when pointing out ways an individual can improve and offer practical solutions for improvement.

5. Correctly Attribute Sources: It's important to accurately attribute information that you share online if it's not a product of your research. Failing to reference information correctly could result in breaching someone else's intellection property add reducing your credence

6. Do Not Spam or Trolls: Do not spam people with messages or comments, especially to people that do not know you. Don't post offensive comments or posts that could make individuals or communities feel uncomfortable. The internet is accessible to anyone, so be conscious of the images and language you use in your texts and comments.

7. Be Professional: Online communication should always maintain a professional standard about the communication's content. Avoid resorting

to impolite language or being emotional when communicating even when the context would seem to call for it. There should always be a distinct line between personal and professional communication, depending on the context.

## Conclusion

In conclusion, digital etiquette is essential, and its quality has significant impacts on relationships individuals make online. Poor digital etiquette affects relationships, performative communication channels in the digital environment, and even mental health. There are general rules to follow to maintain positive and constructive communication and interaction online. Each person has a role to play in creating a positive community online since everyone will benefit from civil and constructive communication.

# Chapter 10

# Listening Skills

Listening is an essential skill that plays a crucial role in our personal and professional lives. The ability to listen actively and attentively can help us build stronger relationships, resolve conflicts, and promote effective communication. In this essay, we will explore the importance of listening skills in different areas of life and provide practical tips for enhancing these skills.

In personal relationships, listening plays a pivotal role in building and maintaining strong bonds between individuals. When we listen actively to our partners, family members, and friends, we communicate that we value their opinions and care about their feelings. This can help foster trust and mutual respect, which are critical components of healthy relationships.

Active listening involves paying attention to what the other person is saying, asking questions to clarify their meaning, and reflecting back what we have heard.

By doing so, we can gain a deeper understanding of the other person's perspective and create a sense of empathy and connection. Additionally, active listening can help prevent misunderstandings and miscommunications that can strain relationships.

In the workplace, listening skills are equally important. Effective communication is essential for achieving organizational goals, managing conflicts, and building strong teams. Listening to colleagues, superiors, and subordinates can help us understand their needs, goals, and concerns and work collaboratively to achieve shared objectives.

Active listening can also help managers foster a positive and productive work environment. By listening to the concerns and feedback of employees, managers can address issues before they escalate, promote transparency and accountability, and build employee morale and loyalty. Furthermore, by actively seeking out diverse perspectives and ideas, managers can create a culture of innovation and adaptability that is essential for staying competitive in today's fast-paced business environment.

Listening skills are also crucial in academic settings. Students who listen actively to their teachers and classmates can develop a deeper understanding of course material, engage in critical thinking, and improve their academic performance. Active listening in an educational setting involves taking notes, asking questions, seeking clarification, and participating in discussions.

Moreover, listening skills can help students navigate social situations and build meaningful relationships with their peers. By actively listening to others' opinions and experiences, students can learn to appreciate diverse perspectives, develop empathy and understanding, and communicate effectively.

In summary, listening skills play an essential role in our personal and professional lives, helping us build relationships, resolve conflicts, and promote effective communication. To enhance our listening skills, we can practice active listening techniques, such as paying attention, asking questions, seeking clarification, and reflecting back what we have heard. Additionally, we can cultivate a mindset of openness and curiosity, seeking out diverse perspectives and ideas and maintaining an attitude of respect and empathy towards others.

Overall, developing strong listening skills can help us succeed in various areas of life, from personal relationships to academic and professional settings. By investing in our listening skills, we can expand our horizons, deepen our relationships, and achieve greater success in all our endeavors.

# Chapter 11

# Self Awareness & Personality

Personality development refers to the process of enhancing and improving various aspects of one's personality. It involves acquiring and developing qualities, skills, attitudes, and behaviors that contribute to personal growth, self-confidence, effective communication, and overall success in life.

Here are some key tips for personality development:

1. Self-awareness: Take the time to understand your strengths, weaknesses, values, and goals. This self-reflection allows you to identify areas for improvement and set personal development goals.
2. Continuous learning: Engage in lifelong learning to broaden your knowledge and skills. Read books, attend workshops, take courses, and seek out opportunities for personal and professional growth.

3. Positive mindset: Cultivate a positive attitude and outlook on life. Practice gratitude, optimism, and kindness towards yourself and others. Surround yourself with positive influences and avoid negative self-talk.

4. Effective communication: Develop strong communication skills, both verbal and non-verbal. Practice active listening, clarity in expression, and empathy in your interactions with others.

5. Emotional intelligence: Enhance your emotional intelligence by understanding and managing your own emotions, as well as empathizing with others. This skill helps build better relationships and enables effective conflict resolution.

6. Time management: Learn to prioritize tasks, set realistic goals, and manage your time effectively. This skill allows you to be more productive, reduce stress, and achieve a better work-life balance.

7. Confidence building: Work on building self-confidence and self-esteem. Celebrate your achievements, step out of your comfort zone, and take on new challenges to boost your confidence levels.

8. Adaptability and resilience: Develop the ability to adapt to change and bounce back from setbacks. Embrace challenges as opportunities for growth and learn from failures.
9. Interpersonal skills: Enhance your social skills, such as teamwork, leadership, and collaboration. Build strong relationships, network with others, and develop effective interpersonal communication.
10. Personal grooming: Pay attention to your physical appearance, hygiene, and personal style. Dress appropriately for different occasions and present yourself in a professional manner.

Remember, personality development is a lifelong journey. It requires consistent effort, self-reflection, and a willingness to grow and improve. Embrace the process, be patient with yourself, and enjoy the rewards of personal growth and development.

Self-awareness is a crucial aspect of personal growth and overall success in life. Here are a few ways self-awareness can contribute to your development:

Identifying strengths and weaknesses: Self-awareness allows you to recognize your strengths, which can be cultivated and leveraged to achieve your goals. It also helps you acknowledge your weaknesses, giving you the opportunity to work on them and improve.

Setting realistic goals: By understanding your abilities, limitations, and values, self-awareness enables you to set realistic and meaningful goals. This helps direct your efforts and resources towards activities that align with your aspirations and give you a sense of purpose.

Improved decision-making: Being self-aware enhances your ability to make effective decisions. When you understand your values, priorities, and goals, you can evaluate options more objectively and make choices that align with your long-term vision.

Building better relationships: Self-awareness helps you understand your emotions, reactions, and communication style. This awareness translates into better interpersonal skills as you become more attuned to the needs and feelings of others. It also allows you to manage conflicts more effectively and build deeper, more authentic connections with people.

Increased self-confidence: Self-awareness brings clarity about who you are and what you stand for. This knowledge fosters self-confidence because you have a strong understanding of your abilities, values, and boundaries. This confidence radiates in your actions and interactions with others, leading to greater success in various areas of life.

Enhancing emotional intelligence: Self-awareness is a cornerstone of emotional intelligence. It helps you recognize and understand your emotions, as well as how they influence your thoughts and behaviors. This awareness enables you to regulate your emotions effectively, handle stress, and empathize with others, all of which contribute to healthier relationships and personal growth.

Continuous self-improvement: Self-awareness fuels a desire for self-improvement and ongoing personal development. It motivates you to seek feedback, learn from your experiences, and continuously strive for growth. With a growth mindset fostered by self-awareness, you are...

Increased resilience: Self-awareness allows you to identify and understand your triggers, stressors, and patterns of behavior. With this awareness, you can develop coping strategies and resilience to navigate challenges and setbacks effectively. You become more adaptable and better equipped to bounce back from difficult situations.

Personal growth and self-improvement: Self-awareness is the foundation for personal growth and self-improvement. By understanding your strengths and weaknesses, you can focus on areas that need improvement and work towards becoming the best version of yourself. This continuous self-reflection and growth contribute to a more fulfilling and meaningful life.

Better self-care: When you are self-aware, you have a deeper understanding of your needs, both physically and mentally. This enables you to prioritize self-care and make choices that support your well-being. You are more likely to engage in activities that bring you joy, nurture your body, and cultivate a positive mindset.

Effective leadership: Self-awareness is a key trait of effective leaders. When you are aware of your own strengths, weaknesses, and emotions, you can lead with authenticity and empathy. You are also more open to feedback and can make necessary adjustments to improve your leadership style.

Developing self-awareness takes time and ongoing effort. It involves practices like self-reflection, introspection, mindfulness, and seeking feedback from others. By cultivating self-awareness, you can unlock your full potential, build meaningful relationships, and lead a more fulfilled life.

Developing self-awareness can indeed help individuals navigate challenges and setbacks more effectively.

Identifying triggers and patterns: Self-awareness allows you to identify your triggers, the things that cause stress or emotional reactions. By understanding what triggers you, you can better prepare for challenging situations and develop strategies to manage your emotions effectively. Additionally, self-awareness helps you recognize patterns of behavior or negative thoughts that may contribute to setbacks. This awareness allows you to break free from those patterns and make positive changes.

Taking responsibility: Self-awareness empowers you to take responsibility for your actions, choices, and outcomes. Instead of blaming external factors, you recognize the role you play in creating your reality. This mindset shift enables you to focus on finding solutions rather than dwelling on the problem. It promotes a proactive approach to challenges, leading to quicker and more effective problem-solving.

Adapting and adjusting: With self-awareness, you gain insights into your strengths, weaknesses, and limitations. This understanding helps you adapt and adjust your approach when faced with obstacles or setbacks. You can leverage your strengths to find alternative solutions or seek support in areas where you may need assistance. Being aware of your limitations allows you to be realistic in your expectations and seek help when necessary.

Building resilience: Self-awareness contributes to building resilience, the ability to bounce back from challenges. When you are self-aware, you can recognize and manage your emotions during difficult times. You become more mindful, developing coping strategies such as practicing self-care, seeking support from others, or engaging in activities that bring you joy. This resilience helps you navigate setbacks with a more positive mindset and bounce back stronger than before.

Learning from experiences: Self-awareness enables you to reflect on your experiences and learn from them. By analyzing what went well and what didn't, you can extract valuable lessons for future challenges. This introspective process allows you to grow and make improvements, making you better prepared to handle similar situations in the future.

Overall, developing self-awareness provides individuals with the tools to understand themselves better, manage their emotions effectively, and make conscious choices during challenging times. It empowers them to take control of their lives and navigate setbacks with resilience and adaptability.

Learning and growth: Self-awareness promotes a growth mindset, where setbacks and challenges are seen as opportunities for learning and personal development. By being aware of your strengths and weaknesses, you can focus on areas that need improvement and actively seek opportunities for growth. You can engage in continuous learning, acquire new skills, and adapt to changing circumstances more effectively.

Effective communication: Self-awareness enhances your communication skills. When you are aware of your emotions, thoughts, and reactions, you can express yourself more clearly and assertively. You can also recognize when your emotions might be affecting your communication and take steps to address them before engaging in conversations. Being aware of your own communication style can also help you better understand and empathize with others, improving your relationships and collaboration during challenging times.

Building meaningful relationships: Self-awareness allows you to understand your values, needs, and boundaries, which are essential in building healthy and meaningful relationships. It helps you navigate difficult conversations or conflicts by expressing yourself authentically without compromising your values. Moreover, self-awareness allows you to recognize and appreciate the unique perspectives and emotions of others, fostering empathy and connection.

Decision-making: Self-awareness plays a crucial role in making sound decisions during setbacks. By understanding your emotions, biases, and core values, you can make decisions that align with your long-term goals and well-being. Self-awareness helps you separate your emotional reactions from objective analysis, enabling you to make rational choices even in challenging situations.

Resolving inner conflicts: Setbacks and challenges often give rise to inner conflicts, such as doubts, fears, or conflicting priorities. Self-awareness helps you identify and resolve these internal conflicts by understanding your motivations, values, and desires. This self-reflection empowers you to make choices that align with your true self and minimize inner turmoil.

Overall, developing self-awareness is a valuable tool for navigating challenges and setbacks. It allows you to understand yourself better, manage your emotions effectively, and make informed decisions that lead to personal growth and resilience.

# Chapter 12

# Self-care

Self-care is an important aspect of maintaining overall well-being and managing the challenges and setbacks life throws our way. It involves taking intentional actions to nurture your physical, mental, and emotional health. Here are some key areas of self-care:

1. Physical self-care: This involves taking care of your body through activities such as regular exercise, eating healthy, getting enough sleep, and practicing good hygiene. Paying attention to your physical needs allows you to have more energy, better focus, and improved overall health.

2. Emotional self-care: Emotional self-care involves recognizing and acknowledging your feelings, and taking steps to nurture your emotional well-being. This can include activities

such as journaling, seeking support from loved ones, engaging in activities that bring you joy, practicing mindfulness or meditation, and creating healthy boundaries.

3. Mental self-care: This encompasses activities that support your mental well-being and cognitive function. It can involve engaging in activities that stimulate your mind, such as reading, learning new skills, participating in puzzles or brain games, and practicing relaxation techniques like deep breathing or meditation.
4. Social self-care: Humans are social creatures, and nurturing connections with others is vital for our well-being. Engaging in social self-care can involve spending quality time with loved ones, joining communities or groups with shared interests, and seeking support or guidance from trusted individuals.
5. Spiritual self-care: This area focuses on nourishing your spiritual beliefs and connecting with something larger than yourself. For some, it may involve religious activities, while for others, it could be spending time in nature, practicing meditation or mindfulness, or engaging in activities that align with their values and personal growth.

Remember, self-care is highly individualized, and what works for one person may not work for another. It's important to listen to your own needs and preferences and find practices that resonate with you. Incorporating self-care into your routine can help you better cope with setbacks, reduce stress, and improve your overall well-being.

How can regular exercise and healthy eating contribute to improved overall well-being?

Regular exercise and healthy eating play crucial roles in improving overall well-being. Here's how they contribute:

1. Physical health: Regular exercise helps maintain a healthy weight, reduces the risk of chronic diseases (such as heart disease, diabetes, and certain cancers), strengthens muscles and bones, improves cardiovascular health, and enhances overall physical fitness. Healthy eating provides the body with essential nutrients, vitamins, and minerals needed for optimal functioning, supports a strong immune system, aids in digestion, and helps maintain a healthy body composition.
2. Mental health: Exercise has been shown to boost mood by increasing the production of endorphins, which are natural mood elevators.

It also reduces symptoms of depression and anxiety, improves cognitive function, enhances sleep quality, and increases self-esteem and body image. Healthy eating, especially a diet rich in fruits, vegetables, whole grains, and omega-3 fatty acids, is associated with lower rates of mental health disorders and improved cognitive function.

3. Energy and vitality: Regular exercise improves energy levels by increasing blood flow and oxygen delivery to the muscles and other tissues. It also helps improve sleep quality, which in turn enhances daytime energy levels. Healthy eating provides the body with the necessary macronutrients and micronutrients that fuel cellular processes, support energy metabolism, and promote vitality.

4. Stress management: Exercise is a natural stress reliever. It helps reduce cortisol levels (the stress hormone) and stimulates the production of endorphins, which can elevate mood and promote relaxation. Healthy eating contributes to stress management by providing the nutrients needed for optimal brain function and regulating blood sugar levels, which can affect mood and stress levels.

5. Longevity and overall quality of life: Regular exercise and healthy eating are associated with a reduced risk of premature death and an improved quality of life. They help prevent and manage chronic diseases, enhance physical functioning, maintain cognitive health, boost immunity, and promote overall well-being.

Incorporating regular exercise and healthy eating habits into your lifestyle can have profound effects on your physical and mental well-being, leading to improved overall quality of life.

# Chapter 13

# Twentieth Century Skills

Twentieth-century skills, also known as 21st-century skills, refer to a set of competencies and abilities that are considered essential for individuals to thrive in the modern world. These skills are often seen as necessary for success in the digital age and in an increasingly interconnected and globalized society. Some examples of Twentieth-century skills include:

1. Critical thinking and problem-solving: The ability to analyze information, evaluate different perspectives, and find innovative solutions to complex problems.

2. Creativity and innovation: The capacity to think creatively, generate new ideas, and approach challenges with originality and flexibility.

3. Communication and collaboration: The skill to effectively express ideas, listen actively, and

work collaboratively with diverse teams to achieve common goals.

4. Information literacy: The ability to identify, evaluate, and effectively use information from various sources, including digital media, while being aware of its credibility, relevance, and ethical use.
5. Digital literacy: The competence to navigate and utilize digital technologies, including computer literacy, online communication, digital content creation, and data analysis.
6. Global and cultural awareness: The understanding and appreciation of diverse cultures, perspectives, and global issues, along with the ability to communicate across cultural boundaries.
7. Adaptability and resilience: The capacity to adapt to changing circumstances, learn from failures, and bounce back from setbacks.
8. Emotional intelligence: The ability to recognize and manage one's own emotions, as well as understand and empathize with others' emotions, leading to effective interpersonal relationships.

9. Leadership and teamwork: The capability to lead and inspire others, delegate tasks, and collaborate effectively within a team.
10. Lifelong learning: The mindset and motivation to continuously learn, acquire new knowledge, and develop new skills throughout one's life.

These Twentieth-century skills are considered critical for individuals to thrive in a rapidly evolving world, where technology, globalization, and the need for innovative thinking and problem-solving are increasingly important in various personal, academic, and professional contexts.

Developing and enhancing critical thinking and problem-solving skills requires practice and intentional effort. Here are some strategies you can use to strengthen these skills:

1. Ask Questions: Encourage curiosity by asking questions about the information you come across. Ask yourself why, how, and what if, to deepen your understanding and challenge assumptions.

2. Analyse Information: Learn to evaluate information critically. Look for evidence, assess credibility, and consider different perspectives and biases. Separate facts from opinions and examine underlying assumptions.

3. Seek Different Perspectives: Engage in discussions with people who have diverse viewpoints. This can help you gain new insights and challenge your own thinking.

4. Solve Real-Life Problems: Look for opportunities to apply critical thinking and problem-solving skills in your everyday life. Break problems down into smaller parts, analyze each part, and explore different possible solutions.

5. Practice Reflection: Regularly reflect on your own thinking processes and decisions. Consider what worked well and what could have been done differently. Reflecting on past experiences helps to improve problem-solving abilities.

6. Learn from Mistakes: Embrace failures as learning opportunities. When faced with challenges or setbacks, analyse what went wrong and identify areas for improvement.

7. Develop Analytical Skills: Read books, articles, and research papers that challenge your thinking. Practice analysing arguments and identifying logical fallacies.

8. Use Technology Wisely: Utilize online resources, educational platforms, and tools that promote critical thinking and problem-solving skills. For example, online puzzles, brain teasers, and

strategy games can help sharpen your cognitive abilities.

9. Collaborate with Others: Engage in group projects or team activities where you can brainstorm ideas, seek feedback, and work together to solve problems. Collaborative environments promote diverse thinking and creative problem-solving.
10. Continuous Learning: Cultivate a growth mindset and have a thirst for knowledge. Stay open to learning new things, exploring different disciplines, and seeking out opportunities for personal and professional development.

Remember, developing critical thinking and problem-solving skills is an ongoing process. By consciously practicing these strategies, you can enhance your ability to think critically and approach problems with a more analytical and creative mindset.

# Chapter 14

# Teachinng Business a Literature in Teaching Business Communication

The use of poetry in business communication teaching can be an innovative and creative way to teach students about the importance of effective communication in the professional world. Despite its perception as being an art form only for literary enthusiasts, poetry has an array of benefits that can enhance communication skills.

Firstly, poetry emphasizes the importance of concise and precise language. The poetic form encourages writers to choose their words carefully, as each word holds weight and significance. This is a crucial skill in business communication, where clarity and brevity are essential. By introducing students to poetry and promoting the practice of using fewer words to convey meaning, they can learn how to make their messages more powerful and impactful.

Secondly, poetry can enhance creativity and imagination. It provides a platform to express oneself freely and creatively. This mindset can apply in business communication, where innovation and creativity are highly valued. Using poetry as a means of generating ideas may help students to think outside the box and develop unique and original ideas for projects or presentations.

Thirdly, poetry can improve critical thinking skills. The analysis of poetic language demands attention to detail and the ability to interpret complex information. These skills are fundamental for business communication, where one must analyze information and interpret it accurately to make important business decisions.

Finally, poetry teaches empathy and emotional intelligence, which are critical components of successful communication in any field. When studying poetry, individuals often put themselves in the shoes of the writer and try to understand their perspectives and experiences. Similarly, in business communication, understanding the viewpoints of clients and colleagues is vital. Studying poetry can foster empathetic communication in the workplace, leading to stronger relationships and better results.

Introducing poetry into business communication teaching can have numerous benefits for students. By emphasizing the importance of concise language, fostering creativity, improving critical thinking skills, and nurturing empathy, poetry can enhance communication skills and help train future leaders in the business world.

There are many great poems that can be used to teach business communication skills. For example, "The Road Not Taken" by Robert Frost can be used to emphasize the importance of decision-making and the consequences of choices in the business world. "Do Not Go Gentle into That Good Night" by Dylan Thomas can be used to illustrate the power of persuasion and negotiation skills. Additionally, poems like "The Waste Land" by T.S. Eliot or "Ode to a Nightingale" by John Keats can be used to improve critical thinking and analysis skills.

Sure, another example could be "Invictus" by William Ernest Henley, which can be used to emphasize resilience and perseverance in the face of challenges, which are important qualities in the business world. "If—" by Rudyard Kipling can be used to illustrate the importance of leadership and ethical decision-making. Overall, there are many poetry examples that can be utilized to teach various business communication skills, depending on the specific focus and needs of the students.

Absolutely! Another example is "To His Coy Mistress" by Andrew Marvell, which can be used to teach persuasion and negotiation skills in romantic and professional settings. "Hymn to Intellectual Beauty " by Percy Bysshe Shelley can be used to teach critical thinking and analysis skills in the context of innovation and creativity. Finally, "Stopping by Woods on a Snowy Evening" by Robert Frost can be used to teach time management and prioritization skills. These are just a few more examples, but I hope they provide some useful insights into the diverse ways in which poetry can be utilized in teaching business communication skills.

Yes, "The Love Song of J. Alfred Prufrock" by T.S. Eliot can be used to teach effective self-presentation and communication in a professional setting. "The Red Wheelbarrow" by William Carlos Williams can be used to teach the importance of concise language and effective use of imagery. "The Charge of the Light Brigade" by Alfred, Lord Tennyson can be used to teach strategic thinking and decision-making under pressure. These are just a few additional examples, but there are countless other poems that can be applied to specific areas of business communication.

Yes, there are many other literary works that can be used to teach business communication skills. For example, plays such as "Death of a Salesman" by Arthur Miller can be used to teach effective sales techniques and interpersonal communication in a business setting. Novels like "The Great Gatsby" by F. Scott Fitzgerald can be used to teach the importance of networking and socializing in business, while also highlighting the dangers of excess and materialism. These are just a few additional examples, but there are countless other literary works that can be applied to various aspects of business communication.

Short stories like "The Gift of the Magi" by O. Henry can be used to teach effective negotiation and conflict resolution skills in a business context. Poems like "The Road Not Taken" by Robert Frost can be used to teach decision-making and risk assessment skills in business. And even children's books like "The Cat in The Hat" by Dr. Seuss can be used to teach creativity and innovation in business communication. The possibilities are endless when it comes to incorporating literature into teaching business communication skills!

Some other classic works of literature that can be used to teach valuable business skills include "The Art of War" by Sun Tzu, which can be applied to strategic planning and decision-making in business. "The Prince" by Niccolo Machiavelli can be used to teach leadership and management skills in a business setting. "To Kill a Mockingbird" by Harper Lee can be used to teach the importance of ethics and integrity in business communication. And "The Odyssey" by Homer can be used to teach effective negotiation and conflict resolution skills in business. These are just a few examples, but there are many other classic works of literature that can be applied to various aspects of business communication and skills development.

Another classic work of literature that can be used to teach valuable business skills is "The Great Gatsby" by F. Scott Fitzgerald. This novel can be used to teach lessons about communication, networking, and the importance of building strong relationships in business. Additionally, "Animal Farm" by George Orwell can be used to teach lessons about power dynamics and effective leadership in a business setting. And finally, "The Catcher in the Rye" by J.D. Salinger can be used to teach lessons about empathy and emotional intelligence in business communication. These are just a few more examples, but there are countless works of literature that can be applied to business skills development.

The use of Information and Communication Technology (ICT) in the classroom has become increasingly common in recent years. ICT refers to the use of digital devices and software to enhance the teaching and learning experience. This can include everything from interactive whiteboards and multimedia presentations to online quizzes and e-learning tools. Here, we will discuss some of the benefits of using ICT in the classroom.

Firstly, the use of ICT can greatly enhance student engagement and motivation. With so much technology available today, students are used to interacting with digital devices and multimedia content. By incorporating ICT into their lessons, teachers can make the learning experience more interactive and engaging, and thus increase student interest and participation. When students are actively engaged in their learning, they are more likely to retain information and develop a deeper understanding of the subject matter.

Secondly, the use of ICT can help to individualize instruction and cater to a wider range of learning styles. With the use of mobile devices and online tools, teachers can provide individualized feedback to each student and tailor their instruction based on their specific needs. This can be especially beneficial for students who require additional support or who have learning disabilities. By utilizing a variety of ICT tools, teachers can provide a more inclusive and diverse learning environment.

Another benefit of using ICT in the classroom is the ease of collaboration and group work. With the use of online tools and platforms, students can work together and share information in real-time. Teachers can also use online tools to facilitate communication and collaboration outside of the classroom, allowing for more productive and efficient group work.

Lastly, the use of ICT can provide teachers with a wealth of resources and materials to enhance their lessons. With online databases and educational software, teachers can access a wide range of multimedia content, including videos, images, and interactive presentations. This can be especially useful for subjects that require visual aids, such as science or geography.

In conclusion, the use of ICT in the classroom has many benefits, including increasing student engagement and motivation, catering to individual learning needs, enabling collaboration and group work, and providing a variety of resources and materials for teachers. As technology continues to advance, it is important for educators to embrace ICT and utilize it in their teaching practices to create a more effective and inclusive learning environment.

Emotional Intelligence: Understanding and Developing Your Emotions

Emotions are a powerful force in human life and they play a significant role in our decision-making, relationships, and overall well-being. Emotional intelligence (EI) is a skill that involves the ability to understand and manage emotions, which has become increasingly important in today's society. In this essay, we'll explore what emotional intelligence is, why it's important, and how you can develop your own emotional intelligence.

## What is Emotional Intelligence?

Emotional intelligence is the ability to recognize, understand, and manage your own emotions, as well as recognizing and understanding the emotions of others. This includes being able to regulate one's reactions to emotions so that they don't negatively impact personal or professional relationships.

## Why is Emotional Intelligence Important?

Emotional intelligence is an essential skill in both personal and professional contexts. In personal relationships, having high emotional intelligence can help individuals navigate complicated emotions that arise in relationships with loved ones. In professional settings, emotional intelligence is critical to effective leadership, teamwork, and overall success in almost any job. Emotional intelligence also helps individuals avoid making impulsive or irrational decisions during moments of high stress.

How to Develop Emotional Intelligence

Developing emotional intelligence is an ongoing process that requires consistent effort. Here are some strategies for improving emotional intelligence:

1. Self-Reflection: One of the fundamental aspects of developing emotional intelligence is being self-reflective. Individuals can take time to identify their emotions and understand how they're feeling in certain situations. This awareness allows individuals to regulate their emotions and adjust their behaviours accordingly.
2. Practice Empathy: Empathy is the ability to understand and share the feelings of other people. By practicing empathy, individuals can better connect with others and anticipate their emotional needs.
3. Active Listening: Active listening involves paying attention to a speaker without interruption or distraction. Individuals who engage in active listening can better understand the emotions and experiences of others.
4. Communicate Effectively: Clear communication is essential for healthy relationships. By communicating effectively, individuals can

avoid misunderstandings and address issues before they escalate.

Emotional intelligence is an essential skill for anyone who wants to succeed in both their personal and professional lives. Developing emotional intelligence takes time and effort, but it's a valuable skill that can pay dividends throughout a lifetime. With self-refl

## Interpersonal Communication: The Art of Effective Interaction

Interpersonal communication is a critical aspect of human interaction that has a significant impact on our daily lives. Communication is key to building relationships, establishing trust, and achieving success in almost every area of life. In this essay, we'll delve into what interpersonal communication is, why it's important, and some strategies for improving your interpersonal communication skills.

Interpersonal communication is the exchange of information between two or more people through verbal and nonverbal means. It involves sending and receiving messages with the goal of achieving mutual understanding. It can take many forms, such as face-to-face conversations, phone calls, emails, and text messages.

Interpersonal communication is essential for building and maintaining relationships, whether they are personal or professional. It helps individuals express their thoughts, feelings, and needs in a clear and effective manner. By practicing good interpersonal communication, individuals can establish trust, avoid misunderstandings, and resolve conflicts in a positive way. Effective interpersonal communication skills are also critical to leadership and teamwork, both of which are crucial in many professional contexts.

Strategies for Improving Interpersonal Communication Skills:

Here are five practical strategies for improving interpersonal communication skills:

1. Active Listening: Active listening is a crucial component of effective interpersonal communication. It involves paying attention to what the other person is saying, asking questions for clarification, and demonstrating empathy and understanding.
2. Nonverbal Communication: Nonverbal communication can be just as important as verbal communication in interpersonal interactions

## Introduction

Dyadic communication is a form of interpersonal communication that involves the exchange of information between two individuals. It can take many forms, such as face-to-face conversations, phone calls, emails, and text messages. Dyadic communication plays an essential role in human interaction, serving as a means for building and maintaining relationships, expressing thoughts and feelings, and accomplishing tasks. In this essay, we'll delve into what dyadic communication is, why it's important, and some strategies for improving your dyadic communication skills.

## What is Dyadic Communication?

Dyadic communication is a type of interpersonal communication that takes place between two individuals. It is characterized by a sender and a receiver who exchange messages with the goal of achieving mutual understanding. Dyadic communication can be verbal or nonverbal, and it can take many different forms, such as face-to-face conversations, phone calls, emails, and text messages.

## Why is Dyadic Communication Important?

Dyadic communication is critical for building and maintaining relationships. It provides an opportunity for individuals to express their thoughts, feelings, and needs to another person. By engaging in dyadic communication, individuals can establish trust, avoid misunderstandings, and resolve conflicts in a positive way. Effective dyadic communication skills are also crucial in many professional contexts, as they enable individuals to work collaboratively, provide feedback, and accomplish tasks effectively.

## Strategies for Improving Dyadic Communication Skills

Here are five practical strategies for improving dyadic communication skills:

1. Active Listening: Active listening is one of the most crucial components of effective dyadic communication. It involves paying close attention to what the other person is saying, asking questions for clarification, and reflecting back what you've heard to ensure mutual understanding. Active listening requires both focus and effort, but it's a skill that can be developed over time with practice.

2. Empathy: Empathy is the ability to understand and share the feelings of another person. It's an essential component of effective dyadic communication, as it allows individuals to connect with others on a deeper level. By...

3. Nonverbal Communication: Nonverbal communication refers to the use of body language, facial expressions, and tone of voice to convey meaning. It's an essential aspect of dyadic communication, as it can often communicate more than words alone. Developing awareness of your nonverbal cues and learning to interpret those of others can help improve your dyadic communication skills.
4. Flexibility: Flexibility is crucial to effective dyadic communication. It involves being open to different perspectives, adapting to changing circumstances, and adjusting your communication style to fit the situation. Being flexible can help prevent misunderstandings and facilitate smoother interactions.
5. Clear Communication: Clear communication involves expressing yourself in a concise and direct manner. It's important to be clear about your thoughts, feelings, and needs when engaging in dyadic communication. Avoid using vague or ambiguous language, as this can lead to misunderstandings. Instead, focus on communicating your message clearly and effectively.

## Conclusion

Dyadic communication is a critical aspect of human interaction that plays a vital role in building and maintaining relationships, expressing thoughts and feelings, and accomplishing tasks. Effective dyadic communication skills require active listening, empathy, nonverbal communication, flexibility, and clear communication. Developing these skills takes time and effort, but it's a worthwhile endeavor that can enhance your personal and professional relationships.

Corporate communication and general communication are two types of communication that can differ in their purpose, audience, and mode of delivery.

## Corporate Communication

Corporate communication refers to the communication activities that take place within an organization and between organizations. It is a strategic function that involves the creation, management, and dissemination of messages intended to inform, educate, persuade, and build relationships with stakeholders. Corporate communication typically includes formal modes of communication such as press releases, annual reports, and internal memos. Its primary goal is to project a positive image of the organization and its products or services.

## General Communication

General communication, on the other hand, refers to communication that takes place in everyday life. It encompasses a broad range of interpersonal, group, and mass communication activities. Unlike corporate communication, general communication is not necessarily driven by a specific organizational goal. Instead, it aims to exchange information and build relationships among individuals and groups. General communication can take many forms, including face-to-face conversations, phone calls, emails, text messages, social media posts, and public speeches.

While corporate communication and general communication have some differences, they both play critical roles in our personal and professional lives. Effective communication skills, whether in a corporate or a general setting, are essential for building relationships, managing conflicts, and achieving goals.

Scientific communication is a specialized form of communication that involves the exchange of information among scientists, researchers, and other professionals in scientific fields. It plays an essential role in advancing scientific knowledge and promoting collaboration among researchers.

Scientific communication takes many forms, including peer-reviewed journal articles, conference presentations, posters, and seminars. The primary goal of scientific communication is to disseminate research findings, new ideas, and advancements and to provide a platform for discussion and critique.

One important aspect of scientific communication is that it follows a set of established protocols and conventions. For example, writing a scientific paper or presenting at a scientific conference typically follows a standard structure and format that has been widely adopted by the scientific community. This ensures that the information being shared is clear, concise, and presented in a way that allows others to replicate the study or build upon its findings.

Good scientific communication also requires an understanding of the audience. For instance, a scientific paper may be targeted at a highly specialized audience of experts in a particular field, while a conference presentation may be geared toward a broader audience that includes researchers from different disciplines.

In summary, scientific communication is crucial for promoting scientific progress, open discussion, and collaboration among researchers. Effective scientific communication requires adhering to established conventions and understanding the audience's needs to make the research accessible and understandable to others in the field.

Certainly! Creative communication is a form of communication that combines imaginative thinking, innovative ideas, and artistic expression to convey a message or idea. It is an approach to communication that seeks to engage and provoke an emotional response from the audience, rather than simply delivering information.

Creative communication can take many forms, including advertising campaigns, graphic design, multimedia presentations, video productions, and social media marketing. The goal of creative communication is to capture the audience's attention and inspire them to take action.

To create effective creative communication, it is important to have a deep understanding of the target audience, their interests, and preferences. Messages and designs should be tailored to the audience, using language, visuals, and aesthetics that resonate with them.

A key component of creative communication is storytelling. Storytelling allows brands or organizations to communicate their message in a way that is relatable, memorable, and emotionally engaging. Through storytelling, brands can create a narrative and connect with the audience on a personal level, building trust and loyalty.

Overall, creative communication is an essential tool for brands, organizations, and individuals looking to convey a message in a unique and compelling way. It involves combining imagination, innovation, and artistic expression to create a powerful message that resonates with the audience and inspires action.

There are many different types of communication, each with its own unique characteristics and goals. Here are some of the most common communication types:

1. Verbal communication: This is the most common form of communication, which involves the use of spoken words. Verbal communication can take place both in person and remotely, such as through phone or video calls.
2. Nonverbal communication: This type of communication includes body language, gestures, facial expressions, tone of voice, and other nonverbal cues that convey meaning. Nonverbal communication is often used to supplement or reinforce verbal communication.
3. Written communication: This type of communication includes any form of written message, such as emails, letters, memos, reports, and social media posts. Written communication

can be used for both personal and professional purposes.

4. Visual communication: This includes any type of communication that uses visual elements to convey a message, such as graphic design, branding, photography, and videography. Visual communication is often used in advertising and marketing.
5. Interpersonal communication: This type of communication takes place between two or more people and is focused on building and maintaining relationships. Examples include conversations between friends and family members, as well as business networking.
6. Mass communication: This refers to the distribution of information to large audiences through various mass media channels, such as television, radio, newspapers, and the internet. Mass communication is often used for advertising, public relations, and journalism purposes.

These are just a few of the many different types of communication. Each type has its own strengths and weaknesses and is best suited for different situations. Effective communication requires choosing the right type of communication for the situation, as well as using inappropriately.

## Legal communication

It is a specialized area of communication that involves the communication of legal information, often between lawyers and their clients, or between lawyers and other professionals in the legal system. Legal communication can take many forms, including written documents, oral arguments, negotiations, and courtroom presentations.

Some examples of legal communication include:

1. Legal briefs: Written documents that provide an argument in favor of a particular legal position or interpretation of the law.
2. Contracts: Written agreements that outline the terms of a legal transaction, such as a business deal or employment agreement.
3. Depositions: Oral statements made under oath as part of the pre-trial discovery process in a lawsuit.
4. Courtroom arguments: Oral arguments presented to a judge or jury in a court of law.
5. Settlement negotiations: Discussions between parties involved in a legal dispute to try to reach a mutually acceptable resolution without going to trial.

Effective legal communication requires a thorough knowledge of the law, as well as strong communication skills to effectively convey legal concepts and arguments to others.

## Scientific communication

It is a specialized form of communication that involves the dissemination of scientific information to various audiences, such as scientists, policymakers, and the public. It includes a wide range of activities, such as writing scientific papers, giving presentations at scientific conferences, and explaining scientific findings to the general public.

Some examples of scientific communication include:

1. Scientific papers: Written documents that report on scientific research and are published in scientific journals.
2. Conference presentations: Oral presentations given at scientific conferences to share research findings with other scientists.
3. Science journalism: The communication of scientific discoveries to the general public through news articles, blogs, and other media.

4. Science education: Teachings about science and scientific concepts to students at all academic levels.

Effective scientific communication requires the ability to effectively communicate complex scientific concepts to individuals with varying levels of knowledge and experience. It also involves the use of clear and concise language, accurate data, and appropriate visual aids to convey scientific findings to various audiences.

## Social media communication

It refers to the use of social media platforms, such as Facebook, Twitter, Instagram, LinkedIn, and others, to communicate with a large audience. Social media has become a ubiquitous part of modern life, and it plays an important role in many aspects of communication.

Some examples of social media communication include:

1. Personal messaging: Direct communication between individuals through social media platforms.
2. Status updates: Short messages or posts that allow users to share updates about their lives, thoughts, and activities.

3. Sharing content: Sharing and reposting articles, videos, images, and other content with others on social media.
4. Advertising: Promoting products, services, or brands through targeted advertising on social media.
5. Influencer marketing: Collaborations between marketers and influencers to promote products or services to the influencer's followers.

Effective social media communication requires an understanding of the platform and the target audience, as well as the ability to develop engaging and compelling content. It also involves building and maintaining relationships with followers and responding to feedback in a timely and appropriate manner.

## Technical communication

It is a type of communication that is used to convey technical or specialized information to a specific audience. This can include communicating about technology, engineering, science, or other technical subjects. Technical communication can take many different forms, including written documents, videos, presentations, and more.

Some examples of technical communication include:

1. User manuals: Documents that provide instructions on how to use a particular product or service.
2. Technical reports: Documents that provide detailed information about a technical subject, including research findings, data analysis, and recommendations.
3. Presentations: Visual aids, such as PowerPoint slides or diagrams, that are used to communicate technical information to an audience.
4. Training materials: Documents and resources that are designed to help people learn about a particular subject or technology.
5. Proposals: Documents that outline a proposed plan for a project or initiative, including the technical details and requirements.

Effective technical communication requires both technical expertise and strong communication skills. Technical communicators must be able to translate complex technical information into language that is understandable and relevant to the intended audience. They must also be skilled in using various communication tools and technologies to effectively convey their message.

## Spiritual communication

It is the process of connecting with a higher power, spirit guides, or other spiritual beings to receive guidance, support, and messages. It can take many forms, including prayer, meditation, divination practices, and other spiritual practices.

Some examples of spiritual communication include:

1. Prayer: Communicating with a higher power through spoken or silent words to request guidance, support, or intervention.
2. Meditation: Connecting with one's inner self or the universe to receive guidance and insights through quiet reflection.
3. Divination practices: Using tools such as tarot cards, pendulums, or runes to communicate with spirit guides or receive messages from the universe.
4. Rituals and ceremonies: Conducting specific rituals or ceremonies to create a sacred space for spiritual communication.
5. Dreams: Receiving messages and insights through dreams that provide guidance and direction.

Effective spiritual communication requires an open mind, a willingness to listen and receive messages, and a strong connection to one's spiritual beliefs and practices. It is important to approach spiritual communication with respect and humility, and to seek guidance from trusted source sand knowledgeable practitioners.

Verbal communication is the process of exchanging information through spoken words. It is one of the most common forms of communication that we use in our daily lives, and it can take many different forms depending on the situation and context.

Some examples of verbal communication include:

1. Conversations: Exchanging ideas and information with another person or group through spoken words.
2. Presentations: Delivering information to an audience through a speech or lecture.
3. Phone calls: Communicating with someone over the phone through spoken words.
4. Meetings: Discussing ideas, making decisions, and sharing information with a group of people through spoken words.
5. Interviews: Answering questions and providing information in a one-on-one setting through spoken words.

Effective verbal communication requires clear and concise language, good listening skills, and the ability to adapt to one's audience and situation. It is important to speak clearly and confidently, maintain eye contact, and engage actively with the listener to ensure that the message is received and understood.

## Nonverbal communication

It is the process of exchanging information without using words. It includes all the forms of communication that do not involve speaking or writing, such as body language, facial expressions, hand gestures, tone of voice, eye contact, and posture.

Some examples of nonverbal communication include:

1. Facial expressions: Smiling, frowning, raising eyebrows, and other facial movements can communicate a range of emotions and attitudes.
2. Body language: Posture, gestures, and movement of the arms, hands, and legs can convey confidence, nervousness, enthusiasm, or boredom.
3. Tone of voice: The pitch, volume, and intonation of the voice can provide clues about our mood, emotions, and attitude towards others.

4. Eye contact: Looking into someone's eyes can establish a connection and convey trust, sincerity, or interest.5. Proximity: The distance between people can communicate different levels of intimacy, dominance, or respect. Nonverbal communication can be powerful and can influence how others perceive us and respond to us. It is important to be aware of our own nonverbal cues and to interpret them accurately in others. Developing strong nonverbal communication skills can enhance our ability to connect with others and build effective relationships.

## Phatic communication

It refers to the use of language and other forms of communication that are used to establish social relationships and maintain social bonds rather than convey information or ideas. It is a type of communication that serves a social function rather than an informational one.

Phatic communication can take many different forms, including:

1. Greetings: Saying hello, asking how someone is doing, and exchanging pleasantries are examples of phatic communication that help establish a friendly tone and build rapport.

2. Small talk: Engaging in casual conversation about topics such as the weather, sports, or current events can help establish common ground and build a sense of connection between individuals.

3. Expressions of politeness: Saying "please" and "thank you," holding open doors, and offering compliments are examples of phatic communication that express respect and consideration for others.

4. Social rituals: Participating in shared cultural traditions such as holidays, religious ceremonies, or special occasions can strengthen social bonds and reinforce common values.

Phatic communication may seem superficial or unnecessary, but it plays an important role in establishing and maintaining social connections, especially in informal or unfamiliar settings. By engaging in phatic communication, we signal our interest in building relationships, and we create opportunities for more meaningful interactions in the future. Relationship communication refers to the exchange of information, emotions, and attitudes between individuals in an intimate relationship, such as a romantic partnership or close friendship. Effective relationship communication is critical for building strong, healthy relationships, resolving conflicts, and maintaining trust.

Key elements of effective relationship communication include:

1. Active listening: Listening attentively to your partner's words, thoughts, and feelings is crucial for understanding their perspective and responding with empathy.
2. Assertiveness: Communicating your own needs, wants, and boundaries clearly and respectfully is essential for maintaining a sense of autonomy and self-respect within the relationship.
3. Nonverbal communication: Paying attention to your partner's body language, facial expressions, and tone of voice can provide important clues about their emotional state and help you respond appropriately.
4. Conflict resolution: Conflicts are a natural part of any relationship, but learning to resolve them constructively through active listening, compromise, and problem-solving can help strengthen the relationship rather than tearing it apart.
5. Emotional support: Expressing care, concern, and empathy for your partner during times of

stress, sadness or celebration is important for building trust and intimacy in the relationship.

Effective relationship communication takes practice and effort, but the rewards are well worth it. By communicating openly, honestly, and respectfully with your partner, you can build a stronger, more resilient relationship that is better able to weather the challenges and uncertainties of life.

## Conflict resolution communication

It refers to the strategies and techniques used to manage and resolve conflicts between individuals or groups. Effective conflict resolution communication can help prevent conflicts from escalating into more serious problems, maintain healthy relationships, and promote mutual understanding and respect.

Some key principles of effective conflict resolution communication include:

1. Active listening: Listening attentively to the other person's perspective, without interrupting or judging, is a critical first step in resolving a conflict.

2. Empathy: Trying to understand the other person's feelings and point of view can help defuse anger and frustration and create a more constructive dialogue.

3. Respectful communication: Using respectful, non-blaming language and avoiding personal attacks or insults can help keep the conversation focused on the issue at hand and reduce defensiveness.

4. Compromise: Finding a mutually acceptable solution or compromising on a particular issue can help both parties feel heard and respected, and it can often be the best way to move forward.

5. Problem-solving and negotiation: Collaboratively working through the problem and finding a mutually beneficial solution through negotiation and creative problem-solving can be an effective way to resolve conflicts.

Effective conflict resolution communication takes practice and patience, but it is a skill well worth cultivating. By approaching conflicts with a mindset of openness and respect, and by using effective communication strategies, you can build stronger, more positive relationships and avoid unnecessary conflicts.

## Relationship communication

It refers to the exchange of information, emotions, and attitudes between individuals in an intimate relationship, such as a romantic partnership or close friendship. Effective relationship communication is critical for building strong, healthy relationships, resolving conflicts, and maintaining trust.

Key elements of effective relationship communication include:

1. Active listening: Listening attentively to your partner's words, thoughts, and feelings is crucial for understanding their perspective and responding with empathy.
2. Assertiveness: Communicating your own needs, wants, and boundaries clearly and respectfully is essential for maintaining a sense of autonomy and self-respect within the relationship.
3. Nonverbal communication: Paying attention to your partner's body language, facial expressions, and tone of voice can provide important clues about their emotional state and help you respond appropriately.
4. Conflict resolution: Conflicts are a natural part of any relationship, but learning to resolve them constructively through active listening, compromise, and problem-solving can help strengthen the relationship rather than tearing it apart.

5. Emotional support: Expressing care, concern, and empathy for your partner during times of stress, sadness or celebration is important for building trust and intimacy in the relationship.

Effective relationship communication takes practice and effort, but the rewards are well worth it. By communicating openly, honestly, and respectfully with your partner, you can build a stronger, more resilient relationship that is better able to weather the challenges and uncertainties of life.

Conflict resolution communication refers to the strategies and techniques used to manage and resolve conflicts between individuals or groups. Effective conflict resolution communication can help prevent conflicts from escalating into more serious problems, maintain healthy relationships, and promote mutual understanding and respect.

Some key principles of effective conflict resolution communication include:

1. Active listening: Listening attentively to the other person's perspective, without interrupting or judging, is a critical first step in resolving a conflict.

2. Empathy: Trying to understand the other person's feelings and point of view can help

defuse anger and frustration and create a more constructive dialogue.

3. Respectful communication: Using respectful, non-blaming language and avoiding personal attacks or insults can help keep the conversation focused on the issue at hand and reduce defensiveness.
4. Compromise: Finding a mutually acceptable solution or compromising on a particular issue can help both parties feel heard and respected, and it can often be the best way to move forward.
5. Problem-solving and negotiation: Collaboratively working through the problem and finding a mutually beneficial solution through negotiation and creative problem-solving can be an effective way to resolve conflicts.

Effective conflict resolution communication takes practice and patience, but it is a skill well worth cultivating. By approaching conflicts with a mindset of openness and respect, and by using effective communication strategies, you can build stronger, more positive relationships and avoid unnecessary conflicts.

## Emotional Intelligence: Understanding and Developing Your Emotions

Emotions are a powerful force in human life and they play a significant role in our decision-making, relationships, and overall well-being. Emotional intelligence (EI) is a skill that involves the ability to understand and manage emotions, which has become increasingly important in today's society. In this essay, we'll explore what emotional intelligence is, why it's important, and how you can develop your own emotional intelligence.

### What is Emotional Intelligence?

Emotional intelligence is the ability to recognize, understand, and manage your own emotions, as well as recognizing and understanding the emotions of others. This includes being able to regulate one's reactions to emotions so that they don't negatively impact personal or professional relationships.

### Why is Emotional Intelligence Important?

Emotional intelligence is an essential skill in both personal and professional contexts. In personal relationships, having high emotional intelligence can help individuals navigate complicated emotions that arise in relationships with loved ones. In professional settings, emotional intelligence is critical to effective leadership, teamwork, and overall success in almost any job. Emotional intelligence also helps individuals avoid making impulsive or irrational decisions during moments of high stress.

## How to Develop Emotional Intelligence

Developing emotional intelligence is an ongoing process that requires consistent effort. Here are some strategies for improving emotional intelligence:

1. Self-Reflection: One of the fundamental aspects of developing emotional intelligence is being self-reflective. Individuals can take time to identify their emotions and understand how they're feeling in certain situations. This awareness allows individuals to regulate their emotions and adjust their behaviors accordingly.
2. Practice Empathy: Empathy is the ability to understand and share the feelings of other people. By practicing empathy, individuals can better connect with others and anticipate their emotional needs.
3. Active Listening: Active listening involves paying attention to a speaker without interruption or distraction. Individuals who engage in active

listening can better understand the emotions and experiences of others.

4. Communicate Effectively: Clear communication is essential for healthy relationships. By communicating effectively, individuals can avoid misunderstandings and address issues before they escalate.

## Conclusion:

Emotional intelligence is an essential skill for anyone who wants to succeed in both their personal and professional lives. Developing emotional intelligence takes time and effort, but it's a valuable skill that can pay dividends throughout a lifetime. With self-reflection, empathy, active listening, and effective communication, anyone can develop their emotional intelligence and become a more emotionally intelligent person.

Perception can have a powerful impact on communication and work. Let me provide you with an example to illustrate this.

Suppose there is a workplace where employees from different cultural backgrounds work together. Among them, there is an employee named John, who comes from the United States, and another employee named Aziz, who comes from Saudi Arabia. They both work on the same project and need to communicate regularly to coordinate their work.

John believes in being direct and straightforward in his communication style, while Aziz takes a more indirect approach. John perceives Aziz's indirect communication as vague and unclear, while Aziz perceives John's direct communication as confrontational and impolite.

One day, John sends an email to Aziz requesting a status update on a project. Aziz feels offended by the tone of the message and thinks that John is questioning his competence. As a result, Aziz responds to the email with a defensive and passive-aggressive tone.

John receives Aziz's response and feels frustrated and confused. He thinks that Aziz is not being straightforward and is avoiding answering his question. This leads to a breakdown in communication between John and Aziz, which affects the progress of the project they are working on.In this scenario, the different perceptions of John and Aziz impacted their communication and work. If John had understood Aziz's communication style and taken the time to build a relationship with him, he would have been less likely to perceive his communication as defensive or ambiguous. Similarly, if Aziz had understood John's communication style, he would have been less likely to perceive it as confrontational.To avoid such situations, it is important to be aware of our own perceptions and biases and actively seek to understand others' perspectives. By doing so, we can avoid misunderstandings and work together more effectively towards a common goal.

## Chromatics

Communication is a broad field that encompasses various forms of communication, including verbal, nonverbal, and visual communication. One of the important aspects of visual communication is Chromatics. Chromatics or color theory is the science of colors, their properties, and their interaction with each other. The use of colors in communication is a critical factor that can evoke emotions, create a visual hierarchy, and affect the overall tone and mood of the message. This essay discusses the importance of Chromatics as an aspect of communication.

## The science of colors

Color is perceived by our eyes when light is reflected from an object. The human eye can perceive millions of different hues of color, which are created by the presence of different wavelengths of light. Color psychology suggests that colors can evoke specific emotions and moods. For example, red can elicit feelings of excitement, passion, and love, while blue can evoke a sense of calmness, trust, and authority.

Understanding the science of colors is important for effectively using them in communication.

## Visual communication

Visual communication is the conveyance of a message through visual elements such as images, icons, and graphics. It is a vital aspect of communication because it can be processed faster than other forms of communication. Visual cues are also more engaging and can help to make a message more memorable. The use of color in visual communication is an essential element that can convey meaning, evoke emotions, and influence behavior.

## The role of Chromatics in branding

Branding is the process of creating a unique identity for a product or service. Colors play a significant role in branding because they can help to differentiate a brand from its competitors. Companies often use specific colors in their branding to create a visual identity and convey a certain image. For example, Coca-Cola uses red in its logo and packaging to create a sense of excitement and energy, while IBM uses blue to convey a sense of trust and reliability. The use of Chromatics in branding can influence consumer behavior and create emotional connections between consumers and brands.

The use of Chromatics in marketing and advertising:

Marketing and advertising are crucial aspects of business because they help to promote products and services to a targeted audience. The use of colors in marketing and advertising can help to attract attention, create interest, and influence consumer behavior. For example, fast-food companies often use bright colors such as red and yellow to create a sense of urgency and excitement, while luxury brands such as Chanel often use black and white to convey elegance and sophistication. Colors can also be used to create contrast and emphasize certain elements of an advertisement, such as a call-to-action button.

## Chromatics in web design

Web design is another area where Chromatics plays an essential role. Websites can use color to create a visual hierarchy, guide the user's eye, and create a sense of balance. For example, the use of complementary colors can help to create contrast and make important elements stand out. The use of color can also affect the user's mood and behavior. Studies have shown that websites with warmer colors such as orange and yellow tend to evoke more positive emotions than cooler colors such as blue and green.

## Chromatics in art and design

Art and design are areas where Chromatics is particularly important. Colors can be used to create mood, atmosphere, and meaning in a work of art or design. For example, the use of dark colors such as black and grey can create a sense of mystery and drama, while bright colors can evoke feelings of happiness and joy. Colors can also be used to create contrast, harmony, and balance in a work of art or design.

## Conclusion

In conclusion, Chromatics is a crucial aspect of communication that can influence emotions, behaviors, and attitudes. Understanding the science of colors and their interactions is important for effectively using them in communication. The use of Chromatics in branding, marketing, web design, art, and design is a critical factor that can differentiate a product or service, create emotional connections, and evoke a sense of meaning and purpose. Therefore, it is important for communicators to consider Chromatics when creating visual messages.

## Chronemics

### Introduction

Chronemics is the study of how time affects communication. It involves the way people perceive and use time to communicate, the meanings attached to time, and the effects of time on message interpretation and social relationships. Chronemics can be classified into different forms, including personal time, socio-cultural time, psychological time, and past, present, and future time orientations. This essay discusses the importance of chronemics as an aspect of communication.

## Personal time

Personal time refers to an individual's perception of time and how they manage it. Personal time can vary between individuals, cultures, and settings. For example, in some cultures, punctuality is highly valued, while in others, tardiness is acceptable. Personal time can affect communication in various ways, such as when someone arrives late to a meeting, causing delays or frustration.

## Socio-cultural time

Socio-cultural time refers to time norms established by a particular culture, community, or society. It includes formal and informal time rules, such as scheduled time for work, leisure, social events, and communication. Socio-cultural time can affect communication in various ways, such as determining the appropriate time for business negotiations, religious ceremonies, social gatherings, and even timing for meals.

## Psychological time

Psychological time refers to an individual's perception of time in relation to their emotions, thoughts, and experiences. It involves cognitive processes such as anticipation, recollection, attention, and evaluation. Psychological time can affect communication in various ways, such as when someone is preoccupied with a personal problem, making them unavailable for communication or when someone is too focused on a task, reducing their ability to attend to communication.

## Past, present, and future time orientations

Time orientation refers to an individual's perspective on the past, present, and future. It can have a significant impact on communication since it affects the meaning of language and nonverbal cues. For example, someone with a future time orientation may focus on planning and goal-setting, while someone with a past time orientation may focus on tradition and preservation of culture. Communication differences might arise between these individuals, as one may be perceived as too focused on planning, while the other may be perceived as too nostalgic.

## Effects of chronemics on communication

Chronemics is critical for effective communication since it can influence message interpretation and social relationships. It can affect communication in several ways, including:

1. Time perception: Different people have different time perceptions, which can affect communication, especially when there are different expectations or deadlines. Understanding the time perceptions of others helps to minimize misunderstandings and ensure that communication is effective.

2. Time management: The ability to manage time effectively can affect communication in several ways, such as influencing punctuality and productivity. Good time management skills can help to minimize delays, increase efficiency, and improve communication.

3. Nonverbal cues: Chronemics affects nonverbal cues, such as eye contact, posture, and gestures. For example, someone who is preoccupied with their thoughts may avoid eye contact, while someone who is attentive may maintain eye contact. Understanding nonverbal cues can help to interpret messages better and improve communication.

4. Social relationships: Chronemics affects social relationships since it influences the way people interact with one another. For example,

punctuality is highly valued in some cultures and can be interpreted as a sign of respect or disrespect. Understanding socio-cultural norms around time helps to build positive social relationships and avoid misunderstandings.

## Conclusion

Chronemics is a vital aspect of communication, as it influences how people perceive and use time to communicate. Personal time, socio-cultural time, psychological time, and past, present, and future time orientations are all relevant to understanding chronemics in communication. Understanding the effects of chronemics on communication can help to minimize misunderstandings, improve productivity, and build positive social relationships. Effective communication requires an understanding of chronemics and the ability to navigate its complexities.

Interactions and building lasting relationships.

Formal communication refers to the type of communication that is used in a professional or business setting. This can include communication between colleagues, clients, customers, or other stakeholders. Here are a few characteristics of formal communication:

1. Standard language: Formal communication often requires the use of standard language that is appropriate for the context. This means using proper grammar, vocabulary, and syntax to ensure clarity and accuracy.
2. Structured format: Formal communication often follows a structured format, such as letters, reports, or presentations. These formats may have specific sections or headings that help organize the information and make it easier to understand.
3. Professional tone: Formal communication generally requires a professional tone that reflects the seriousness of the situation or topic being discussed. This means avoiding slang, jokes, or informal language that may be inappropriate for the context.
4. Clear purpose: Formal communication should have a clear purpose or objective. This means identifying the reason for the communication and focusing on the information or message that needs to be conveyed.
5. Respectful attitude: Formal communication requires a respectful attitude towards the person or people being addressed. This means using proper titles, addressing people appropriately,

and avoiding confrontational or disrespectful language.

Overall, formal communication is an important aspect of professional and business settings, and it is important to understand how to communicate effectively in these contexts. By following these characteristics, we can ensure that our communication is clear, accurate, and appropriate for the situation.

A sales team leader was tasked with presenting the company's latest product to potential clients. The team leader created a formal presentation using slides with clear headings and images to support the message. They practiced the presentation ahead of time and used a professional tone and language throughout the presentation.

In all these examples, the communication was formal and followed the characteristics I mentioned earlier, such as a structured format, professional tone, and clear purpose. These case studies demonstrate how effective communication can lead to successful outcomes in business and professional settings.

Sure, here's an essay on digital communication:

# Chapter 15

# Digital Communication: Transforming the Way We Connect

Digital communication has revolutionized the way we connect and interact with each other. With the rise of communication technologies like email, social media, messaging apps, video conferencing, and more, we have entered a new era of connectivity. These digital tools have made it possible for people to communicate instantly and effortlessly, breaking down barriers of time and distance. In this essay, we will explore the impact of digital communication on our personal and professional lives.

One of the most significant impacts of digital communication is its ability to connect people from all over the world. With social media platforms like Facebook, Twitter, and Instagram, people can easily connect and stay in touch with family and friends regardless of their location. This has led to a more global community, where people can share experiences, ideas, and cultures with others.

In the business world, digital communication has transformed the way companies operate. With email and instant messaging, employees can communicate more efficiently and quickly, even if they are located in different parts of the world. Video conferencing technology has also made it possible for remote workers to participate in meetings and conferences, eliminating the need for travel and saving time and money.

However, digital communication has also raised some concerns about privacy and security. With the increase in online communication, there is a risk of sensitive information being leaked or stolen. Cybersecurity is now a major concern for individuals, businesses, and governments alike.

Another concern is the potential negative impact of social media on mental health. The constant stream of information and the pressure to present a perfect image can lead to anxiety and stress. It is important to use social media responsibly and take breaks when needed.

In conclusion, the rise of digital communication has transformed the way we connect with each other, both personally and professionally. It has connected people from all over the world, allowed for more efficient business operations, and created a more global community. However, we must also be aware of the potential risks and take steps to protect our privacy and mental health.

Suppose there is a workplace where employees from different cultural backgrounds work together. Among them, there is an employee named John, who comes from the United States, and another employee named Aziz, who comes from Saudi Arabia. They both work on the same project and need to communicate regularly to coordinate their work.

John believes in being direct and straightforward in his communication style, while Aziz takes a more indirect approach. John perceives Aziz's indirect communication as vague and unclear, while Aziz perceives John's direct communication as confrontational and impolite.

One day, John sends an email to Aziz requesting a status update on a project. Aziz feels offended by the tone of the message and thinks that John is questioning his competence. As a result, Aziz responds to the email with a defensive and passive-aggressive tone.

John receives Aziz's response and feels frustrated and confused. He thinks that Aziz is not being straightforward and is avoiding answering his question.

This leads to a breakdown in communication between John and Aziz, which affects the progress of the project they are working on. In this scenario, the different perceptions of John and Aziz impacted their communication and work. If John had understood Aziz's communication style and taken the time to build a relationship with him, he would have been less likely to perceive his communication as defensive or ambiguous. Similarly, if Aziz had understood John's communication style, he would have been less likely to perceive it as confrontational. To avoid such situations, it is important to be aware of our own perceptions and biases and actively seek to understand others' perspectives. By doing so, we can avoid misunderstandings and work together more effectively towards a common goal.

Communication is the process of exchanging information, ideas, thoughts, and feelings between individuals or groups. It involves the transmission and reception of messages through various channels like verbal, nonverbal, written, or visual means. Effective communication skills are crucial for success in personal relationships, professional life, and societal interactions.

## Types of Communication

1. Verbal Communication:
   - Oral Communication: Involves spoken words, speeches, presentations, conversations.
   - Written Communication: Involves written words, emails, letters, memos, reports.
2. Nonverbal Communication:
   - Body Language: Gestures, facial expressions, postures, eye contact.
   - Tone of Voice: The way words are spoken, tone, volume, pitch, intonation.
   - Facial Expressions: Smiles, frowns, raised eyebrows, nods, pouts.
   - Proxemics: Use of personal space, distance, and physical proximity.
3. Visual Communication:
   - Graphic Communication: Charts, graphs, diagrams, illustrations, images.
   - Presentations: Slides, videos, multimedia elements to convey information.
   - Signage: Symbols, signs, posters, banners for guiding or conveying messages.

4. Listening Skills:

   - Active Listening: Paying full attention, being present, and engaging in the conversation.
   - Empathetic Listening: Understanding others' perspectives, feelings, and emotions.
   - Reflective Listening: Paraphrasing, summarizing, and confirming understanding.

5. Written Communication:

   - Formal Writing: Reports, proposals, official documents using appropriate language.
   - Informal Writing: Emails, texts, instant messaging, with a more conversational tone.
   - Clear and concise writing, proper grammar, punctuation, and formatting.

6. Interpersonal Communication:

   - One-on-One Communication: Conversations between two individuals.
   - Group Communication: Discussions, meetings, collaborations involving multiple people.
   - Conflict Resolution: Negotiating and resolving conflicts in a constructive manner.

7. Cross-Cultural Communication:
    - Communication across different cultures, languages, and social norms.
    - Cultural sensitivity, awareness of etiquette, and respecting diverse perspectives.

Remember, effective communication involves not only conveying messages but also active listening, understanding the audience, adapting to different communication styles, and being aware of nonverbal cues. Developing strong communication skills can enhance relationships, improve teamwork, and foster success in various aspects of life.

The introduction of AI-powered chatbots, such as ChatGPT, has certainly had an impact on the job market. While chatbots can automate certain tasks and improve efficiency in customer service and support, they have also led to changes in job roles and responsibilities. Here are some ways in which ChatGPT and similar technologies have influenced jobs:

1. Customer Service: ChatGPT has been employed in customer service to handle routine customer inquiries and provide instant responses. This automation has reduced the need for human agents to address repetitive and simple queries, freeing them up to focus on more complex and critical customer issues. As a result, customer

service roles have shifted towards higher-level problem-solving and providing personalized assistance.

2. Chatbot Development and Maintenance: The rise of chatbots has created a demand for professionals skilled in developing and maintaining these conversational AI systems. Job roles such as chatbot developers, AI trainers, and conversational designers have emerged as specialized positions in the field of AI and natural language processing. These professionals are responsible for training the AI models, improving the chatbot's conversational capabilities, and ensuring its effectiveness and accuracy.

3. Data Analysis and Insights: ChatGPT generates a vast amount of data from user interactions, which can be analyzed to gain insights into customer behavior, preferences, and pain points. Data analysts and data scientists play a crucial role in extracting meaningful information from this data and using it to drive business decisions, improve customer experiences, and optimize chatbot performance. These roles have become increasingly important in leveraging the potential of AI-powered chatbots.

4. Human Oversight and Quality Assurance: While chatbots are capable of handling many customer inquiries, they may still encounter limitations and issues. Human oversight and quality assurance teams are responsible for monitoring chatbot interactions, identifying errors or inaccuracies, and ensuring that the chatbot operates within ethical and legal boundaries. These roles are instrumental in maintaining the quality and reliability of chatbot interactions.

5. Adaptation and Upskilling: With the introduction of chatbots, some job roles may become obsolete or require adaptation. It is crucial for individuals to upskill and embrace new technologies and tools to remain relevant in the changing job market. This might involve acquiring knowledge in AI, machine learning, natural language processing, or developing skills in areas that complement the capabilities of chatbots.

In summary, while ChatGPT and similar technologies have impacted certain job roles, they have also created new opportunities and transformed existing positions. It is essential for individuals and organizations to adapt, upskill, and leverage the benefits of these technologies to enhance productivity and provide better customer experiences.

## Gen Z communication style

Generation Z, commonly referred to as Gen Z, refers to individuals born between the mid-1990s and early 2010s. As a generation that has grown up in a highly connected digital era, Gen Z has developed a distinct communication style characterized by various factors:

1. Digital Native: Gen Z is known for being digital natives, having grown up with technology and the internet as an integral part of their lives. They are adept at using various digital platforms and prefer communication channels like social media, instant messaging apps, and video calls.
2. Multitasking: Due to the constant exposure to information and technology, Gen Z has become skilled at multitasking. They often engage in multiple conversations simultaneously, switch quickly between different apps or platforms, and tend to have shorter attention spans.
3. Short-form Communication: Gen Z tends to prefer concise and to-the-point communication. They often rely on abbreviations, acronyms, and emojis to express themselves quickly and efficiently. Platforms like Twitter and Snapchat, with their character or time-limited formats, have influenced this preference for brevity.

4. Visual Content: Gen Z embraces visual content such as images, videos, and memes. They appreciate visually appealing and engaging content that can convey messages quickly. Platforms like Instagram, TikTok, and YouTube are popular among Gen Z for their visual nature and easy accessibility.

5. Authenticity: Gen Z values authenticity in communication. They appreciate honesty, transparency, and genuine connections. This generation often seeks real-time updates and unfiltered content, gravitating towards influencers and content creators who share their personal experiences and opinions openly.

6. Social Justice Advocacy: Gen Z is passionate about social issues and actively engages in activism through various online platforms. They use social media to raise awareness, advocate for change, and join causes they believe in. Gen Z's communication style often reflects their desire for inclusivity, representation, and social justice.

7. Memes and Humor: Gen Z has a unique sense of humor heavily influenced by internet memes and viral trends. They enjoy using humor as a form of communication and self-expression,

often sharing memes, GIFs, and humorous content to connect with others.

It's important to note that communication styles can vary among individuals within a generation, and not all Gen Z individuals may exhibit these characteristics. However, these tendencies provide a broad overview of the communication style commonly associated with Gen Z.

Certainly! Here are a few more characteristics of Gen Z's communication style:

8. Memes and Humor: Gen Z has a strong affinity for memes and humor in their communication. Memes, often shared through social media, serve as a way to express emotions, relate to shared experiences, and convey messages in a light-hearted and relatable manner.
9. Collaborative Communication: Gen Z values collaboration and enjoys participating in group conversations and co-creating content. They often use group chats, online forums, and collaborative platforms to exchange ideas, brainstorm, and work together on projects.
10. Personal Branding: Gen Z is conscious of personal branding and self-presentation online. They curate their social media profiles

carefully to showcase their interests, skills, and personality. Building an online presence and connecting with others who share similar passions is important to Gen Z.

11. Socially Conscious Language: Gen Z tends to be conscious of inclusive and politically correct language. They actively use gender-neutral terms, avoid offensive or discriminatory language, and promote equality and respect in their communication.

12. Instant Gratification: Due to the instant nature of digital communication, Gen Z is accustomed to receiving immediate responses and expects quick replies in their conversations. They may feel frustrated with delays in response or if conversations are not fast-paced.

13. Privacy Concerns: As a generation that has experienced the proliferation of personal information online, Gen Z values privacy and tends to be cautious about sharing too much personal information. They are more likely to take steps to protect their privacy, such as using privacy settings and being mindful of what they share online.

It is important to note that while these characteristics are often associated with Gen Z's communication style, there are variations within the generation, and individual preferences may differ. Additionally, communication styles can evolve over time, influenced by cultural shifts and technological advancements.

Certainly! Here are a few additional characteristics of Gen Z's communication style:

14. Emojis and GIFs: Gen Z frequently uses emojis and GIFs to enhance their messages and convey emotions. These visual elements add a layer of expression and playfulness to their digital conversations.

15. Shortened and Abbreviated Language: Gen Z often relies on abbreviations, acronyms, and shortened phrases in their communication. This shorthand helps them save time and fits well with the fast-paced nature of digital conversations.

16. Visual and Multimedia Content: Gen Z engages heavily with visual and multimedia content in their communication. They prefer using platforms like Instagram, Snapchat, and TikTok, which allow them to share and consume images, videos, and stories.

17. Hyperlinks and Sharing: Gen Z is skilled at quickly finding and sharing information online.

They often include hyperlinks to articles, videos, or other sources to support their statements or share interesting content with others.

18. Authenticity and Real-Time Updates: Gen Z values authenticity and real-time updates in their communication. They prefer instant messaging platforms and social media channels that provide live updates and real-time interactions.

19. Response Diversity: Gen Z embraces different response methods in their communication. They might use a combination of text, voice messages, video calls, or even live streaming to interact with others, depending on the context and their personal preferences.

20. Self-Expression: Gen Z sees communication as a way to express their individuality and creativity. They often experiment with different mediums, filters, and effects to make their messages unique and visually appealing.

21. Social Activism: Gen Z is known for its strong advocacy for social causes. They use their communication skills to raise awareness, promote activism, and engage in discussions about important issues such as climate change, equality, and mental health.

It's important to remember that these characteristics are not exclusive to Gen Z and can be observed in different degrees across other generations as well. Each individual's communication style is also influenced by their cultural background, personal experiences, and technological proficiency.

How to bridge the skill gap

Certainly! Here are a few more strategies to bridge the skill gap:

1. Continuous Feedback and Performance Evaluation: Regularly assess employee performance and provide constructive feedback to help them identify areas for improvement. This feedback loop can be invaluable for identifying skill gaps and providing targeted training or development opportunities.
2. Encourage Innovation and Creativity: Foster a culture of innovation and creativity within your organization. Encourage employees to think outside the box, take risks, and develop new skills to adapt to a changing environment. This can help bridge skill gaps and drive organizational growth.
3. Engage in Industry Partnerships: Collaborate with industry associations, professional organizations, and other companies in your

sector. This allows for knowledge sharing, best practices exchange, and collaborative initiatives to address skill gaps collectively.

4. Utilize Technology and Automation: Leverage technology and automation to streamline processes, increase efficiency, and reduce reliance on manual labor. This frees up employees to focus on developing higher-level skills that require human input and creativity.
5. Employee Engagement and Retention Strategies: Invest in employee engagement and retention strategies to attract and retain top talent. This includes providing competitive compensation packages, offering growth opportunities, recognizing and rewarding achievements, and creating a positive work environment.
6. Stay Ahead of Trends: Continuously monitor industry trends and emerging technologies to anticipate future skill requirements. This helps you stay proactive in bridging skill gaps and ensures your organization remains competitive.
7. Measure Success: Regularly evaluate the effectiveness of your skill gap bridging initiatives. This can be done through metrics such as employee performance, productivity, and the ability to meet organizational goals.

Adjust your strategies as needed to maximize impact.

Remember, bridging the skill gap is an ongoing process that requires commitment and adaptability. By implementing these strategies, you can cultivate a skilled workforce capable of driving innovation and achieving long-term success.

Continuous feedback and performance evaluation play a crucial role in identifying and addressing skill gaps in an organization. Here's how they contribute:

1. Identifying Skill Gaps: Through regular feedback and performance evaluations, managers can assess employee performance against the desired skill set for their roles. They can identify areas where employees may be lacking certain skills or competencies required to meet job expectations.
2. Providing Constructive Feedback: Feedback sessions provide an opportunity for managers to communicate the specific areas where an employee needs improvement. This feedback can help employees become aware of their skill gaps and understand the steps they need to take to bridge them.
3. Setting Development Goals: Based on the identified skill gaps, managers can work with

employees to set development goals. These goals can be focused on acquiring the necessary skills and knowledge through training, mentoring, or on-the-job learning. By setting clear goals, employees have a roadmap to address their skill gaps.

4. Tailoring Training and Development Programs: Skill gaps identified through performance evaluations can guide the design and implementation of training and development programs. These programs can be customized to address specific skills or competencies that are lacking in the organization.

5. Individualized Learning Plans: Continuous feedback allows managers and employees to create individualized learning plans to address skill gaps. These plans can include targeted training courses, workshops, job rotations, or other developmental activities that align with the employee's career goals and the organization's needs.

6. Career Progression and Succession Planning: Skill gap identification helps in succession planning and career progression by identifying employees who show potential but have specific skill gaps. Organizations can then develop

talent pipelines to fill critical roles by providing targeted development opportunities to close those gaps.

7. Monitoring Skill Improvement: Continuous feedback and performance evaluation allow managers to monitor the progress made in bridging skill gaps. Regular check-ins and evaluations provide a measure of how well employees are developing the required skills and meeting their development goals. Overall, continuous feedback and performance evaluation provide essential insights into skill gaps, enable targeted development plans, and facilitate the growth and improvement of employees in an organization.

Organizations can tailor their training and development programs to address specific skill gaps identified through performance evaluations in several ways:

1. Customized Training Modules: Organizations can create custom training modules that specifically target the skills and competencies identified as gaps in the performance evaluation process. These modules can be designed to address the unique needs of different roles and departments within the organization.

2. Role-Specific Training Programs: Instead of a one-size-fits-all approach, organizations can develop role-specific training programs that focus on the skills needed for each position. This ensures that employees receive training that directly relates to their job responsibilities and helps them improve in the areas where they are lacking.

3. Mentoring and Coaching Programs: Pairing employees with experienced mentors or coaches who excel in the areas they need to improve can be an effective way to address skill gaps. Mentors can provide guidance, support, and personalized feedback to help employees develop the necessary skills.

4. On-the-Job Training and Job Rotation: Organizations can implement on-the-job training programs or job rotations to provide employees with hands-on experience and exposure to different tasks and responsibilities. This can help them gain the skills needed to fill skill gaps and expand their knowledge base.

5. E-Learning Platforms and Online Courses: Digital learning platforms and online courses offer a flexible and accessible way for employees to acquire new skills. Organizations can

leverage these platforms to provide targeted training materials and resources to address specific skill gaps.

6. Cross-Functional Collaboration and Projects: Encouraging cross-functional collaboration and involvement in projects outside of an employee's immediate role can help them gain exposure to different skills and perspectives. This type of experiential learning can be effective in addressing skill gaps and promoting professional growth.
7. Continuous Feedback and Performance Coaching: Alongside formal training programs, organizations should incorporate continuous feedback and performance coaching. Regular check-ins, coaching sessions, and feedback loops allow managers to provide ongoing guidance and support to employees as they work on improving their skills.

By tailoring training and development programs to address specific skill gaps, organizations can ensure that employees receive targeted support and opportunities for growth, leading to improved performance and overall organizational success.

To ensure that custom training modules effectively target identified skill gaps and meet the unique needs of different roles and departments within an organization, organizations can follow these steps:

1. Conduct a Needs Assessment: Before developing any custom training module, it is essential to conduct a thorough needs assessment. This involves gathering data through employee surveys, interviews, focus groups, and performance evaluations to identify specific skill gaps and training needs. The needs assessment should take into account the unique requirements of different roles and departments within the organization.

2. Involve Stakeholders: It is crucial to involve stakeholders, such as managers, supervisors, and employees, in the process of designing and developing custom training modules. Their input will provide valuable insights into the specific skills and competencies required for each role or department.

3. Align Training Objectives with Organizational Goals: Custom training modules should align with the overall organizational goals and objectives. By connecting the training content to the strategic goals of the organization, employees will see the relevance of the training and be motivated to learn and apply the newly acquired skills.

4. Use Performance Data: Utilize performance data, such as performance evaluations, KPIs, and feedback from supervisors, to identify specific areas where employees are struggling or lacking in skills. This data can help to focus the training content on the most critical skills that need improvement.

5. Customize Content and Delivery Methods: Custom training modules should be tailored to the specific needs and preferences of different roles and departments. This includes adapting the content, delivery methods, and learning materials to suit the learning styles, job requirements, and schedules of employees. For example, sales teams may benefit from interactive simulations, while technical teams may prefer hands-on practical exercises.

6. Provide Ongoing Support: Custom training modules should not be standalone events. To ensure effectiveness, organizations should provide ongoing support to employees after the training. This can include follow-up sessions, assessments, coaching, and access to additional resources and materials to reinforce learning and provide opportunities for practice and application of new skills.

7. Evaluate and Revise: Regularly evaluate the effectiveness of the custom training modules through assessments, feedback, and performance metrics. This feedback should be used to revise and improve the training content and delivery methods continuously.

By following these steps, organizations can ensure that their custom training modules effectively target identified skill gaps and meet the unique needs of different roles and departments within the organization.

1. Engage Subject Matter Experts (SMEs): Collaborate with subject matter experts from within the organization or external consultants who have expertise in the specific skills being targeted for training. SMEs can provide valuable insights, expertise, and guidance in designing and developing the custom training modules.
2. Develop Clear Learning Objectives: Each custom training module should have clear and measurable learning objectives that outline what participants should be able to do or know after completing the training. These objectives will guide the development of the content and activities within the module.
3. Choose Appropriate Training Methods: Select training methods and activities that best suit

the learning objectives, content, and target audience. This could include a combination of instructor-led training, e-learning modules, on-the-job training, role plays, case studies, and group discussions, among others. Be mindful of the different learning styles and preferences of employees when deciding on the training methods.

4. Design Engaging and Interactive Content: Make the training content engaging and interactive to enhance knowledge retention and application. Incorporate multimedia elements, such as videos, graphics, and interactive exercises, to make the learning experience more dynamic and effective.

5. Pilot and Evaluate: Before rolling out the custom training module organization-wide, pilot it with a select group of employees to gather feedback and make necessary improvements. Then, evaluate the effectiveness of the training by measuring the impact on employee performance, behavior change, and skill improvement. Use this feedback to refine and enhance the training module as needed.

6. Continuous Improvement: Custom training modules should not be seen as one-time projects.

Instead, organizations should continually assess the effectiveness of the training and make necessary updates and improvements based on evolving needs and feedback from employees.

By following these steps, organizations can develop tailored and effective custom training modules that address specific skill gaps and meet the unique needs of different roles and departments within the organization.

Engaging subject matter experts (SMEs) in the design and development of custom training modules is crucial to ensure the content is accurate, relevant, and effective. Here are some steps organizations can take to effectively engage SMEs:

1. Identify the Right SMEs: Determine the specific skills or knowledge areas required for the training modules and identify SMEs who have expertise in those areas. These could be individuals within the organization, such as experienced employees, trainers, or managers, or external consultants with specialized knowledge.
2. Define Roles and Expectations: Clearly communicate the roles and expectations to the SMEs involved. Let them know how their expertise will contribute to the training module's

development, such as providing subject matter expertise, reviewing content, or conducting training sessions. Establish a clear timeline and deliverables for their involvement.

3. Involve SMEs from the Beginning: Engage SMEs right from the initial stages of the training module's design. Include them in brainstorming and planning sessions to gather their insights and perspectives. Their input can help shape the curriculum, learning objectives, and overall structure of the training modules.

4. Collaborate on Content Development: Work closely with the SMEs to develop the training content. Schedule regular meetings or workshops to discuss and refine the content. Leverage their expertise to ensure accuracy, relevance, and depth of the material. Encourage the SMEs to share real-life examples, case studies, or best practices that can enrich the training experience.

5. Review and Feedback: Seek regular feedback from SMEs throughout the development process. Share drafts of the training modules and invite their input and suggestions for improvement. This collaborative review process will help to incorporate their expertise

and ensure the content aligns with the intended learning outcomes.

6. Pilot Testing: Include SMEs in piloting the training modules with a small group of employees. This will allow them to observe and evaluate the effectiveness of the content and delivery methods. Encourage SMEs to provide feedback based on their observations and make necessary adjustments before the final rollout.
7. Recognition and Appreciation: Acknowledge the contributions of SMEs by recognizing their expertise and effort. Provide appropriate recognition, such as mentioning their involvement in training materials or publicly acknowledging their contribution during training sessions. This recognition will not only validate their expertise but also motivate them to continue contributing to future training initiatives.

By following these steps, organizations can effectively engage SMEs in the design and development of custom training modules, ensuring that the content is accurate, relevant, and beneficial for employees' learning and development.

1. Pilot Testing: Include SMEs in the pilot testing phase of the training modules. This allows

them to experience the content firsthand and provide valuable feedback on its effectiveness. They can identify any areas that need further clarification or improvement based on their expertise and knowledge.

2. Provide Resources and Support: Ensure that SMEs have access to the necessary resources and support throughout the process. This may include providing them with relevant research materials, tools, or technology needed for content development. Address any concerns or challenges they may have and offer assistance when needed.

3. Recognize and Appreciate SMEs: Acknowledge the contribution of SMEs and express gratitude for their involvement in the training module development. Recognize their expertise and the value they bring to the organization. This can be done through verbal recognition, certificates of appreciation, or other forms of acknowledgment.

4. Maintain Ongoing Communication: Keep the lines of communication open with SMEs even after the training modules are developed. They may have additional insights or updates that can enhance the modules over time. Regularly

check-in with them to gather feedback and ensure the content remains up-to-date.

5. Evaluate and Improve: Continuously evaluate the effectiveness of the training modules and gather feedback from learners and SMEs. Use this feedback to make improvements and enhancements to the content. Engage SMEs in the evaluation process to understand their perspective on the training's impact and identify areas for further improvement.

By effectively engaging SMEs in the design and development of custom training modules, organizations can create high-quality, impactful training programs that meet the specific needs of their learners. The expertise and input of SMEs ensure that the content is accurate, relevant, and aligned with the desired learning outcomes.

## Personality Development

Personality development refers to the process of enhancing and improving various aspects of one's personality. It involves acquiring and developing qualities, skills, attitudes, and behaviors that contribute to personal growth, self-confidence, effective communication, and overall success in life.

Here are some key tips for personality development:

1. Self-awareness: Take the time to understand your strengths, weaknesses, values, and goals. This self-reflection allows you to identify areas for improvement and set personal development goals.

2. Continuous learning: Engage in lifelong learning to broaden your knowledge and skills. Read books, attend workshops, take courses, and seek out opportunities for personal and professional growth.

3. Positive mindset: Cultivate a positive attitude and outlook on life. Practice gratitude, optimism, and kindness towards yourself and others. Surround yourself with positive influences and avoid negative self-talk.

4. Effective communication: Develop strong communication skills, both verbal and non-verbal. Practice active listening, clarity in expression, and empathy in your interactions with others.

5. Emotional intelligence: Enhance your emotional intelligence by understanding and managing your own emotions, as well as empathizing with others. This skill helps build better relationships and enables effective conflict resolution.

6. Time management: Learn to prioritize tasks, set realistic goals, and manage your time effectively. This skill allows you to be more productive, reduce stress, and achieve a better work-life balance.

7. Confidence building: Work on building self-confidence and self-esteem. Celebrate your achievements, step out of your comfort zone, and take on new challenges to boost your confidence levels.

8. Adaptability and resilience: Develop the ability to adapt to change and bounce back from setbacks. Embrace challenges as opportunities for growth and learn from failures.

9. Interpersonal skills: Enhance your social skills, such as teamwork, leadership, and collaboration. Build strong relationships, network with others, and develop effective interpersonal communication.

10. Personal grooming: Pay attention to your physical appearance, hygiene, and personal style. Dress appropriately for different occasions and present yourself in a professional manner.

Remember, personality development is a lifelong journey. It requires consistent effort, self-reflection, and a willingness to grow and improve. Embrace the process, be patient with yourself, and enjoy the rewards of personal growth and development.

Self-awareness is a crucial aspect of personal growth and overall success in life. Here are a few ways self-awareness can contribute to your development:

1. Identifying strengths and weaknesses: Self-awareness allows you to recognize your strengths, which can be cultivated and leveraged to achieve your goals. It also helps you acknowledge your weaknesses, giving you the opportunity to work on them and improve.

2. Setting realistic goals: By understanding your abilities, limitations, and values, self-awareness enables you to set realistic and meaningful goals. This helps direct your efforts and resources towards activities that align with your aspirations and give you a sense of purpose.

3. Improved decision-making: Being self-aware enhances your ability to make effective decisions. When you understand your values, priorities, and goals, you can evaluate options morc objectively and make choices that align with your long-term vision.

4. Building better relationships: Self-awareness helps you understand your emotions, reactions, and communication style. This awareness

translates into better interpersonal skills as you become more attuned to the needs and feelings of others. It also allows you to manage conflicts more effectively and build deeper, more authentic connections with people.

5. Increased self-confidence: Self-awareness brings clarity about who you are and what you stand for. This knowledge fosters self-confidence because you have a strong understanding of your abilities, values, and boundaries. This confidence radiates in your actions and interactions with others, leading to greater success in various areas of life.

6. Enhancing emotional intelligence: Self-awareness is a cornerstone of emotional intelligence. It helps you recognize and understand your emotions, as well as how they influence your thoughts and behaviors. This awareness enables you to regulate your emotions effectively, handle stress, and empathize with others, all of which contribute to healthier relationships and personal growth.

7. Continuous self-improvement: Self-awareness fuels a desire for self-improvement and ongoing personal development. It motivates you to seek feedback, learn from your experiences, and

continuously strive for growth. With a growth mindset fostered by self-awareness, you are...

Sure, here are a few more benefits of self-awareness:

1. Increased resilience: Self-awareness allows you to identify and understand your triggers, stressors, and patterns of behavior. With this awareness, you can develop coping strategies and resilience to navigate challenges and setbacks effectively. You become more adaptable and better equipped to bounce back from difficult situations.

2. Personal growth and self-improvement: Self-awareness is the foundation for personal growth and self-improvement. By understanding your strengths and weaknesses, you can focus on areas that need improvement and work towards becoming the best version of yourself. This continuous self-reflection and growth contribute to a more fulfilling and meaningful life.

3. Better self-care: When you are self-aware, you have a deeper understanding of your needs, both physically and mentally. This enables you to prioritize self-care and make choices that support your well-being. You are more likely to

engage in activities that bring you joy, nurture your body, and cultivate a positive mindset.

4. Effective leadership: Self-awareness is a key trait of effective leaders. When you are aware of your own strengths, weaknesses, and emotions, you can lead with authenticity and empathy. You are also more open to feedback and can make necessary adjustments to improve your leadership style.

Developing self-awareness takes time and ongoing effort. It involves practices like self-reflection, introspection, mindfulness, and seeking feedback from others. By cultivating self-awareness, you can unlock your full potential, build meaningful relationships, and lead a more fulfilled life.

Developing self-awareness can indeed help individuals navigate challenges and setbacks more effectively. Here's how:

1. Identifying triggers and patterns: Self-awareness allows you to identify your triggers, the things that cause stress or emotional reactions. By understanding what triggers you, you can better prepare for challenging situations and develop strategies to manage your emotions effectively. Additionally, self-awareness helps you recognize patterns of behavior or negative

thoughts that may contribute to setbacks. This awareness allows you to break free from those patterns and make positive changes.

2. Taking responsibility: Self-awareness empowers you to take responsibility for your actions, choices, and outcomes. Instead of blaming external factors, you recognize the role you play in creating your reality. This mindset shift enables you to focus on finding solutions rather than dwelling on the problem. It promotes a proactive approach to challenges, leading to quicker and more effective problem-solving.

3. Adapting and adjusting: With self-awareness, you gain insights into your strengths, weaknesses, and limitations. This understanding helps you adapt and adjust your approach when faced with obstacles or setbacks. You can leverage your strengths to find alternative solutions or seek support in areas where you may need assistance. Being aware of your limitations allows you to be realistic in your expectations and seek help when necessary.

4. Building resilience: Self-awareness contributes to building resilience, the ability to bounce back from challenges. When you are self-aware, you can recognize and manage your emotions

during difficult times. You become more mindful, developing coping strategies such as practicing self-care, seeking support from others, or engaging in activities that bring you joy. This resilience helps you navigate setbacks with a more positive mindset and bounce back stronger than before.

5. Learning from experiences: Self-awareness enables you to reflect on your experiences and learn from them. By analyzing what went well and what didn't, you can extract valuable lessons for future challenges. This introspective process allows you to grow and make improvements, making you better prepared to handle similar situations in the future.

Overall, developing self-awareness provides individuals with the tools to understand themselves better, manage their emotions effectively, and make conscious choices during challenging times. It empowers them to take control of their lives and navigate setbacks with resilience and adaptability.

Learning and growth: Self-awareness promotes a growth mindset, where setbacks and challenges are seen as opportunities for learning and personal development. By being aware of your strengths and weaknesses, you can focus on areas that need improvement and actively seek opportunities for growth. You can engage in continuous learning, acquire new skills, and adapt to changing circumstances more effectively.

6. Effective communication: Self-awareness enhances your communication skills. When you are aware of your emotions, thoughts, and reactions, you can express yourself more clearly and assertively. You can also recognize when your emotions might be affecting your communication and take steps to address them before engaging in conversations. Being aware of your own communication style can also help you better understand and empathize with others, improving your relationships and collaboration during challenging times.

7. Building meaningful relationships: Self-awareness allows you to understand your values, needs, and boundaries, which are essential in building healthy and meaningful relationships. It helps you navigate difficult conversations or conflicts by expressing yourself authentically without compromising your values. Moreover, self-awareness allows you to recognize and appreciate the unique

perspectives and emotions of others, fostering empathy and connection.

8. Decision-making: Self-awareness plays a crucial role in making sound decisions during setbacks. By understanding your emotions, biases, and core values, you can make decisions that align with your long-term goals and well-being. Self-awareness helps you separate your emotional reactions from objective analysis, enabling you to make rational choices even in challenging situations.

9. Resolving inner conflicts: Setbacks and challenges often give rise to inner conflicts, such as doubts, fears, or conflicting priorities. Self-awareness helps you identify and resolve these internal conflicts by understanding your motivations, values, and desires. This self-reflection empowers you to make choices that align with your true self and minimize inner turmoil.

Overall, developing self-awareness is a valuable tool for navigating challenges and setbacks. It allows you to understand yourself better, manage your emotions effectively, and make informed decisions that lead to personal growth and resilience.

## Self care

Self-care is an important aspect of maintaining overall well-being and managing the challenges and setbacks life throws our way. It involves taking intentional actions to nurture your physical, mental, and emotional health. Here are some key areas of self-care:

1. Physical self-care: This involves taking care of your body through activities such as regular exercise, eating healthy, getting enough sleep, and practicing good hygiene. Paying attention to your physical needs allows you to have more energy, better focus, and improved overall health.

2. Emotional self-care: Emotional self-care involves recognizing and acknowledging your feelings, and taking steps to nurture your emotional well-being. This can include activities such as journaling, seeking support from loved ones, engaging in activities that bring you joy, practicing mindfulness or meditation, and creating healthy boundaries.

3. Mental self-care: This encompasses activities that support your mental well-being and cognitive function. It can involve engaging in activities that stimulate your mind, such as reading, learning new skills, participating

in puzzles or brain games, and practicing relaxation techniques like deep breathing or meditation.

4. Social self-care: Humans are social creatures, and nurturing connections with others is vital for our well-being. Engaging in social self-care can involve spending quality time with loved ones, joining communities or groups with shared interests, and seeking support or guidance from trusted individuals.
5. Spiritual self-care: This area focuses on nourishing your spiritual beliefs and connecting with something larger than yourself. For some, it may involve religious activities, while for others, it could be spending time in nature, practicing meditation or mindfulness, or engaging in activities that align with their values and personal growth.

Remember, self-care is highly individualized, and what works for one person may not work for another. It's important to listen to your own needs and preferences and find practices that resonate with you. Incorporating self-care into your routine can help you better cope with setbacks, reduce stress, and improve your overall well-being.

Regular exercise and healthy eating play crucial roles in improving overall well-being. Here's how they contribute:

1. Physical health: Regular exercise helps maintain a healthy weight, reduces the risk of chronic diseases (such as heart disease, diabetes, and certain cancers), strengthens muscles and bones, improves cardiovascular health, and enhances overall physical fitness. Healthy eating provides the body with essential nutrients, vitamins, and minerals needed for optimal functioning, supports a strong immune system, aids in digestion, and helps maintain a healthy body composition.

2. Mental health: Exercise has been shown to boost mood by increasing the production of endorphins, which are natural mood elevators. It also reduces symptoms of depression and anxiety, improves cognitive function, enhances sleep quality, and increases self-esteem and body image. Healthy eating, especially a diet rich in fruits, vegetables, whole grains, and omega-3 fatty acids, is associated with lower rates of mental health disorders and improved cognitive function.

3. Energy and vitality: Regular exercise improves energy levels by increasing blood flow and oxygen delivery to the muscles and other tissues. It also helps improve sleep quality, which in turn enhances daytime energy levels. Healthy eating provides the body with the necessary macronutrients and micronutrients that fuel cellular processes, support energy metabolism, and promote vitality.

4. Stress management: Exercise is a natural stress reliever. It helps reduce cortisol levels (the stress hormone) and stimulates the production of endorphins, which can elevate mood and promote relaxation. Healthy eating contributes to stress management by providing the nutrients needed for optimal brain function and regulating blood sugar levels, which can affect mood and stress levels.

5. Longevity and overall quality of life: Regular exercise and healthy eating are associated with a reduced risk of premature death and an improved quality of life. They help prevent and manage chronic diseases, enhance physical functioning, maintain cognitive health, boost immunity, and promote overall well-being.

Incorporating regular exercise and healthy eating habits into your lifestyle can have profound effects on your physical and mental well-being, leading to improved overall quality of life.

## Skill versus knowledge

Skill and knowledge are two distinct but interconnected concepts.

Knowledge refers to the understanding, information, and awareness that a person possesses about a particular subject or area. It is acquired through learning, education, training, and experience. Knowledge can be theoretical or practical and can be obtained from various sources such as books, teachers, research, and personal exploration.

Skill, on the other hand, refers to the ability to perform specific tasks or activities effectively. It is developed through practice, repetition, and hands-on experience. Skills are more focused on application and performance rather than simply having knowledge about something. Skills require practical proficiency, dexterity, and the ability to execute tasks with precision and efficiency.

While knowledge provides the foundation and understanding of a subject, skill is the practical application of that knowledge. You can have extensive knowledge about a particular field or topic, but without the corresponding skills, you may not be able to effectively apply that knowledge in real-life situations.

For example, you may have extensive knowledge of programming languages, but unless you have the skill to write code and develop software, your knowledge alone may not be enough to be considered a skilled programmer.

In summary, knowledge is the theoretical understanding of a subject, while skill is the practical ability to perform tasks related to that subject. Both knowledge and skill are important and complement each other, as having knowledge enables the development of skills, and skills require a foundation of knowledge to be effectively applied.

One example of a profession or field where extensive knowledge is essential, but skill is not as important could be academia, particularly in research-based positions. In academia, researchers and scholars often focus on acquiring in-depth knowledge in their respective fields of study. They spend significant time studying, analyzing data, conducting experiments, and publishing papers to contribute to the body of knowledge in their area of expertise.

While researchers do need certain skills to carry out their work effectively, such as critical thinking, data analysis, and writing skills, the emphasis is more on knowledge acquisition and intellectual contributions. The ability to think critically, conduct thorough literature reviews, and generate new knowledge through research is often more valued in academia compared to certain practical skills.

However, it is important to note that even in academia, having certain skills can greatly enhance one's effectiveness and impact. For example, presentation skills can help researchers effectively communicate their findings, teaching skills can help them impart knowledge to students, and collaboration skills can facilitate interdisciplinary research projects.

Overall, while there are fields where extensive knowledge is crucial and skills may take a backseat, it is often the combination of both knowledge and skills that leads to success and excellence in any profession.

## Twentieth century skills

Twentieth-century skills, also known as 21st-century skills, refer to a set of competencies and abilities that are considered essential for individuals to thrive in the modern world. These skills are often seen as necessary for success in the digital age and in an increasingly interconnected and globalized society. Some examples of Twentieth-century skills include:

1. Critical thinking and problem-solving: The ability to analyze information, evaluate different perspectives, and find innovative solutions to complex problems.

2. Creativity and innovation: The capacity to think creatively, generate new ideas, and approach challenges with originality and flexibility.

3. Communication and collaboration: The skill to effectively express ideas, listen actively, and work collaboratively with diverse teams to achieve common goals.

4. Information literacy: The ability to identify, evaluate, and effectively use information from various sources, including digital media, while being aware of its credibility, relevance, and ethical use.

5. Digital literacy: The competence to navigate and utilize digital technologies, including computer literacy, online communication, digital content creation, and data analysis.

6. Global and cultural awareness: The understanding and appreciation of diverse cultures, perspectives, and global issues, along with the ability to communicate across cultural boundaries.

7. Adaptability and resilience: The capacity to adapt to changing circumstances, learn from failures, and bounce back from setbacks.

8. Emotional intelligence: The ability to recognize and manage one's own emotions, as well as understand and empathize with others' emotions, leading to effective interpersonal relationships.

9. Leadership and teamwork: The capability to lead and inspire others, delegate tasks, and collaborate effectively within a team.

10. Lifelong learning: The mindset and motivation to continuously learn, acquire new knowledge, and develop new skills throughout one's life.

These Twentieth-century skills are considered critical for individuals to thrive in a rapidly evolving world, where technology, globalization, and the need for innovative thinking and problem-solving are increasingly important in various personal, academic, and professional contexts.

Developing and enhancing critical thinking and problem-solving skills requires practice and intentional effort. Here are some strategies you can use to strengthen these skills:

1. Ask Questions: Encourage curiosity by asking questions about the information you come across. Ask yourself why, how, and what if, to deepen your understanding and challenge assumptions.

2. Analyze Information: Learn to evaluate information critically. Look for evidence, assess credibility, and consider different perspectives and biases. Separate facts from opinions and examine underlying assumptions.

3. Seek Different Perspectives: Engage in discussions with people who have diverse viewpoints. This can help you gain new insights and challenge your own thinking.

4. Solve Real-Life Problems: Look for opportunities to apply critical thinking and problem-solving skills in your everyday life. Break problems down into smaller parts, analyze each part, and explore different possible solutions.

5. Practice Reflection: Regularly reflect on your own thinking processes and decisions. Consider what worked well and what could have been done differently. Reflecting on past experiences helps to improve problem-solving abilities.

6. Learn from Mistakes: Embrace failures as learning opportunities. When faced with

challenges or setbacks, analyze what went wrong and identify areas for improvement.

7. Develop Analytical Skills: Read books, articles, and research papers that challenge your thinking. Practice analyzing arguments and identifying logical fallacies.

8. Use Technology Wisely: Utilize online resources, educational platforms, and tools that promote critical thinking and problem-solving skills. For example, online puzzles, brain teasers, and strategy games can help sharpen your cognitive abilities.

9. Collaborate with Others: Engage in group projects or team activities where you can brainstorm ideas, seek feedback, and work together to solve problems. Collaborative environments promote diverse thinking and creative problem-solving.

10. Continuous Learning: Cultivate a growth mindset and have a thirst for knowledge. Stay open to learning new things, exploring different disciplines, and seeking out opportunities for personal and professional development.

Remember, developing critical thinking and problem-solving skills is an ongoing process. By consciously practicing these strategies, you can enhance your ability to think critically and approach problems with a more analytical and creative minds.

# Chapter 16

# Ememrging Communication Patterns

In 2023, communication patterns have continued to evolve and adapt to the changing technological landscape and societal trends. Here are a few notable communication patterns that have emerged:

1. Digital Communication Dominance: Digital communication platforms such as messaging apps, email, social media, and video conferencing have become the primary means of communication for many people. These platforms offer convenience, speed, and accessibility, allowing individuals to connect with others across distances and time zones.
2. Remote Work and Virtual Collaboration: With the rise of remote work and flexible work arrangements, virtual collaboration tools

have become essential for communication in the workplace. Video conferencing, project management software, and instant messaging platforms enable teams to communicate and collaborate effectively regardless of their physical location.

3. Emphasis on Visual and Multimedia Content: In an age of information overload, visual and multimedia content has gained prominence. People are increasingly using emojis, GIFs, images, and videos to convey emotions, messages, and ideas in a concise and engaging manner.

4. Shorter and More Instantaneous Interactions: Due to the prevalence of instant messaging and social media, communication interactions have become shorter and more instantaneous. People often communicate through brief text messages or posts, and expect quick responses.

5. Increased Awareness of Digital Literacy: As communication relies heavily on digital platforms, there is a growing awareness and emphasis on digital literacy. Skills such as online etiquette, media literacy, and information verification have become crucial for effective and responsible communication in the digital age.

6. Personalization and Targeted Communication: With advances in data analytics and artificial intelligence, communication has become more personalized and targeted. Companies and organizations use customer data to tailor their messaging and content to individual preferences, increasing the relevance and effectiveness of their communication.

7. Emphasis on Emotional Intelligence: With the rise of remote work and digital communication, the importance of emotional intelligence in communication has become more apparent. People are recognizing the significance of empathy, active listening, and understanding emotions in building meaningful connections and resolving conflicts.

8. Personalization and Targeted Communication: With advances in data analytics and artificial intelligence, communication has become more personalized and targeted. Companies and organizations use customer data to tailor their messages and promotions, providing more relevant and engaging content.

9. Rise of Voice Assistants: Voice assistants such as Siri, Alexa, and Google Assistant have gained popularity, allowing users to interact with their devices through voice commands.

These assistants can perform various tasks, including sending messages, making calls, setting reminders, and searching for information.

10. Growing Importance of Privacy and Security: As more personal information is shared online and through digital communication channels, privacy and security have become significant concerns. Users are increasingly aware of the potential risks and are taking steps to protect their data and communications.

11. Influencer Marketing and Social Media Influence: Influencer marketing has become a prominent strategy for brands to reach their target audience. Social media influencers with large followings use their platforms to promote products and services, leveraging their influence and credibility.

12. Real-Time Customer Support: Many companies now offer real-time customer support through chatbots and live chat features. This allows customers to receive immediate assistance and resolve issues efficiently.

13. Remote Learning and Online Education: The COVID-19 pandemic accelerated the adoption of remote learning and online education.

Schools, universities, and training programs have shifted to virtual classrooms and online platforms, enabling students to continue their education remotely.

14. Expansion of Video Communication: Video communication has become essential for work meetings, conferences, and even social interactions. Platforms like Zoom, Microsoft Teams, and Google Meet have seen widespread adoption, allowing people to connect face-to-face virtually.
15. Integration of Artificial Intelligence: Artificial intelligence is being integrated into communication tools and platforms to enhance user experience. AI-powered chatbots, voice recognition, and predictive algorithms help automate tasks and provide personalized recommendations.
16. Collaboration and Team Communication Tools: Collaboration tools like Slack, Microsoft Teams, and Google Workspace have revolutionized how teams communicate and work together. These platforms offer features such as real-time messaging, file sharing, project management, and video conferencing.

17. Emphasis on Visual Content: Visual content, such as images, videos, and infographics, has become increasingly significant in communication. It helps convey messages quickly, engage audiences, and stand out in crowded digital spaces.

These are just a few trends in communication that have emerged in recent years. The rapid pace of technological advancements continues to shape the way we connect and interact with one another.

These are just a few examples of communication patterns that have emerged in 2023. As technology continues to advance and societal norms evolve, communication patterns will likely continue to change and shape our interactions.

www.ingramcontent.com/pod-product-compliance
Lightning Source LLC
La Vergne TN
LVHW041206150826
845673LV00001B/301

* 9 7 9 8 8 9 0 6 6 8 7 1 4 *